*D*OGFISH *I*SLAND

A MEMOIR

DOGFISH ISLAND

A MEMOIR

Robbie Dunlap

Zion Publishing

Cover photo courtesy of Phyllis Dwyer, Longmont, Colorado

A publisher's note: While writing this story, Dunlap struggled with how to refer to the people of color who lived in her childhood community. She writes, "These people I write about nurtured me during difficult years and remain in my memory as generous, warm-hearted friends, whom I still hold with deep affection and gratitude. I refer to them in the way they referred to themselves, as "colored"—a descriptive term used throughout the country during that time. I use this term with deep respect." In addition, the author has changed one or two names for the sake of privacy.

ISBN: 978-1-7333982-7-5
Library of Congress Control Number: 2020915055

Books can be purchased online.
For bulk orders, contact the author
meadowlarkfarm@indra.com

Published by
Zion Publishing
Des Moines, Iowa

for my daughter
Linda

"There is a terrible hunger for love.
We all experience that in our lives—the pain, the loneliness.
We must have the courage to recognize it.
The poor you may have right in your own family.
Find them. Love them."
Mother Teresa

"Forgiveness is the fruit
of understanding."
Thich Nhat Hanh

Contents

Introduction

When I began this memoir, I thought it would be a traditional one, in which a writer's responsibility is simply to tell his or her story as accurately as possible. I was advised that I was writing about what happened to me, and I should feel no obligation to spare others or to shed light on possible reasons for their behavior. "Let the chips fall where they may." One could argue this not only is a writer's privilege but the correct plan for a personal memoir. Yet, I discovered I couldn't settle for this; it resulted in a skewed and unfair story. I could only tell my truth by weaving in my family's truth. Thus, the story of my journey as a young child into early teenage years grew to include the stories of three generations of women in our extended family, as well as my father's story.

For years I lived with the mystery of why our family was so unhappy, why we lived with suffocating silence and so many secrets, and why my father burst into rages at my two older half-sisters. My mother blamed all of this on me, telling me it resulted from my birth. "If only you had never been born," she would say. From childhood, I shouldered the guilt for everyone's misery. It has taken most of my life for me to untangle the complexity behind

Mother's accusation, as well as what lay buried beneath the silence that choked our family. After years of searching and healing, I have attempted to pull the pieces together here.

In spite of my efforts to be accurate, I realize no two people remember the same incident in the same way. I can only state these are my memories as I lived them. Other members of my family might have written parts of our story differently. My hope is that although some of our remembrances may have varied, I have succeeded in going deeper than the details and have captured the truths we shared. I wish there was even one person still alive who could fill the gaps of my information or correct any erroneous conclusions I may have drawn, but I am the only one left who can tell this tale. I trust my story causes no one pain. My intention has been to give back the voices of those who were silenced. If I accomplished this, their underlying innocence and goodness will be revealed.

Real Girl

❧

I first left home on a summer day Mother killed the chicken. I was
not yet three years old. The back door of our house banged as
she strode to the chicken pen, grabbed one of the brown speckled
hens, and took it to the tree stump beside the washhouse, near the
rope swing where I played with my older half-sisters, Marilyn and
Ellin. I climbed out of the swing to watch. She pulled the butcher
knife from the corner of the washhouse and held the neck of the
squawking chicken against the stump. The head fell to the ground;
the eyes turned glassy.

The body ran for a short distance, flopped and floundered,
then righted itself to run once again. Blood spurted from its sev-
ered neck, pulsing in long streams, staining the brown feathers,
splashing against the swing, splashing against the white wall of the
washhouse.

No! No! Head on.

Mother continued to ignore me. She stabbed the knife back
into the wooden frame of the washhouse, wiped her hands on her
faded blue denim apron, and returned to the house. The headless
chicken continued to struggle.

Marilyn stood nearby. She walked to the knife, yanked it free, turned to me and approached, slowly. A rivulet of blood dripped from the blade onto her hand. She bent down, narrowed her gray eyes, and leered. She lowered the knife closer. The flopping of the headless chicken slowed.

"That will be you one day," she hissed. She pressed the blade against my throat. "Just like that stupid chicken. And if you tell …" She chopped the knife in the air, then put it back against my throat. "One day I'm going to get you, you stupid chicken."

I stared into her rage, wanting to move, to back up, to run away, but my body froze, my legs were so heavy.

I stumbled into our empty house and trembled in the middle of the kitchen. Mother and Daddy were working in the greenhouses attached to our house. I wanted Daddy.

Marilyn's voice echoed in my head. "If you tell …"

I turned and lurched out the front door.

✆ ✆ ✆

This was 1936. Our family owned the floral and garden center in Marion, Kansas, a town of 2,300 nestled on the western slope of the Flint Hills. In the 1860s, when homesteaders searching for a fresh start in life traveled west along the Santa Fe Trail, those who approached what would become Marion Centre were stopped by a sheer drop-off of limestone bluffs. These pioneers looked over the valley below and saw a fertile countryside, with a rare, bubbling spring and two long snaking rivers converging there. Most travelers skirted these daunting cliffs and kept going, but those few who realized the value of what they saw met the challenge. They used their oxen to lower wagons and animals down the cliffs by ropes, then led the oxen the long, rugged way down. With the flinty hills at their backs and—beyond this lush valley—a vast, flat, and arid prairie spreading as far west as they could see, these hardy souls knew they had found something precious. They hung a tin dipper beside the spring so the weary and thirsty could drink from this sweet water.

❧ ❧ ❧

By the 1930s, two streets sloped up the limestone bluffs, providing easy access between the hill and valley that together comprised the town by then called Marion. The community was surrounded by rich land fenced off into small family farms. Buildings that would one day be listed on the National Historic Register had been constructed from the native limestone: the Marion County Courthouse, the Hill School building, and the Presbyterian Church.

In 1932, my newlywed parents, who lived in Wheaton, Illinois, also headed west to seek a new life. They tied a mattress on the top of Daddy's dilapidated black coupe, tucked Marilyn and Ellin into the back seat—Mother's daughters, ages seven and five, from her first marriage—and drove to Kansas. They had purchased a greenhouse sight unseen in Marion. They arrived on the Fourth of July and sat in the driveway, peering through rain at what they owned: a weed-infested five acres of land; a greenhouse with a sagging frame, its every pane of glass shattered; and a shabby, attached four-room house. "When we carried the mattress into the house," Mother said, "we couldn't find a dry place to put it. The roof leaked everywhere."

It took all their resources, and an entire year of backbreaking work, to make the repairs necessary to restore the greenhouse before they could plant their first seeds. But then a severe drought hit the area. The clay ground hardened and cracked; nothing grew. The scarce water was rationed. The town's trade, dependent on the harvests of the surrounding farms, shriveled along with the fields. Locals spent money on necessities, not flowers. My parents' income hovered at zero for those two years—the family existing on oatmeal, plus the occasional catfish Daddy caught in Mud Creek. During their second year, I was born. In spite of all their hardships, Mother eagerly anticipated my birth—until I arrived.

◦ ◦ ◦

So much that happened before I was born remained part of the silence that shrouded our lives. Once, during a rare moment when Mother and I were alone, she began reminiscing. Her eyes dulled as she recalled how good Daddy had been to Marilyn and Ellin in the beginning, how he made them broomstick ponies and pushed them in the rope swing he hung from the big walnut tree, how they would drive out to the lake on hot summer nights and lie on blankets to discover shapes of animals among the stars. At last, she had a family for her girls.

Her eyes refocused as her lips tightened. "Everything would have stayed good if only you had never been born."

◦ ◦ ◦

"The worst disappointment of my life," Mother sobbed to the nurses.

They tried to be encouraging: "Look at your beautiful little girl." But she turned her back to stare at the wall, weeping. She spread the word that she wanted to sell me, each day hoping someone would step forward. She offered to swap babies with a woman who gave birth to a boy at the same time, a woman who already had four sons waiting at home. She wept again when the woman refused.

Through the years she would repeat, "When my first child was a girl, I was disappointed. When my second was a girl, I was more disappointed but refused to lose hope. But when that third one was a girl, that was the last straw."

From as early as I can remember, until my mother's death at ninety-three, I listened as she told people her story: "I would have taken a single nickel for her, but no one thought she was worth five cents."

The day Mother was forced to take me home from the hospital, the air turned bitterly cold, unusual for October. The car crunched through an early snow as it entered the driveway. My parents and sisters lived in a four-room house and the living space was reduced down to three when they designated the front living room as the floral shop. Marilyn and Ellin slept on the floor of the living/dining room, while our parents slept in the only bedroom, where Daddy squeezed a crib against the wall. An iron pot-bellied stove heated the house, but that night as the temperatures dipped near zero, no one got up to add wood to the stove.

Mother told me years later that my crying bothered her sleep for hours until I finally shut up. When she went to my crib the next morning, I felt frozen to her touch. She looked sheepish as she described how tiny I looked, dressed only in a soaked diaper with no blanket, unfed, rolled into a silent, still ball.

Mother had made it clear that she resented having to take me home, but how can I understand Daddy's failure to add wood to the stove or respond to my crying? Did he absorb Mother's despair to such a degree that it plunged him into his own immobilizing depression? I'll never know.

Recently, I had a dream in which I observed my first night home from the hospital. I saw myself in my crib, curled up tight. My parents were lying in their bed a few feet away. As I watched, the figure of a woman rose from my infant body and drifted over to my parents, where she covered my mother with a blanket.

I first believed my dream meant that I came into the world knowing that my mother's needs were greater than my own. Later,

I grasped a more full meaning: my birth had broken my mother's spirit. She would never be able to take care of me. That night, my spirit chose not only to live but to bring love, though I knew I would have to survive on my own. And one day I would rise up and take care of her.

ల ల ల

Our home and business were located on Walnut Street, where towering black walnut trees lined the entire length of the street and shadowed the sidewalk. Their roots buckled the cement in places. The day Mother slaughtered that chicken, I tripped over one of those broken places and scraped my knee. I got up and kept going. Although I was not quite three, I feel again the pain of my injured knee and recall the journey with strange vividness. I stepped down and up unfamiliar curbs, crossed red-bricked streets, heard the sounds of car motors, a sharp honk, tires bumping over the bricks, voices walking past. No one stopped me.

Finally, more than a mile from my home, I recognized the black screen door of the grocery store where I would go with Daddy. Two curling sticky strips of brown paper hung near the door covered with struggling flies. An orange cat napped in the sun-filled window, stretched between boxes of tomatoes.

I pushed the door open to a tinkling bell. It felt cool inside; an oscillating fan stirred the air. Mr. Schmersey was sacking potatoes from a bushel basket. He looked up and brightened, wiped his dirty hands on the white towel tied around his waist, brushed the front of his white shirt, and stooped to pick me up.

"Well, well, here's my little girl," he said. I felt his strong arms lifting me, smelled the dusty potatoes, earthy and comforting. I leaned into his warm chest. He glanced toward the door, then looked down into my face, arching his black eyebrows.

He carried me to the counter and sat me beside the giant glass jar filled with sugarcoated lemon drops and tiny Tootsie Rolls. Lifting the lid, he told me to reach inside. As I rummaged for a fist full of lemon drops, the rim of the jar hurt my bare arm, but I ignored it when the sweetness of the candy wafted into my face. He watched my delight, chuckling. I chuckled, too.

"Those brown eyes are smiling today," he teased, his own dark eyes smiling back.

I beamed, swinging my legs back and forth off the edge of the counter, rolling my tongue around my lemon drop. He cranked the handle of the wooden phone box hanging on his wall, lifted the receiver, and spoke into the black mouthpiece. My smile faded; my legs slowed.

Daddy came. He had a silly grin on his face. Standing in the middle of the scuffed wooden floor, he shifted from one foot to the other, reaching his left hand deep into the pocket of his dirty brown work trousers to jingle loose coins. He and Mr. Schmersey glanced at me and shook their heads, laughing.

Daddy lifted me off the counter. I stiffened, reaching both arms for Mr. Schmersey. He put another lemon drop from the candy jar into my hand; I threw it on the floor. I didn't want candy. I wanted him to keep me, not let Daddy take me home where Marilyn waited with the knife, where if she saw me with Daddy, she'd whack off my head.

The bell jingled as Daddy carried me out of the store, opened the car door, pried my hands off the frame, and shoved me inside.

After my adventure that day of going to find my friend Mr. Schmersey, I didn't return to his store again. I understood he would telephone Daddy, who would come and take me home. It would be months before I left home again, but, meanwhile, I didn't stay around Marilyn and Ellin. I remained close to my father—the only place I felt safe.

∾ ∾ ∾

Our house was joined with our family's floral and garden center, so our parents were never far away. When I had grown old enough to follow my daddy around the greenhouse, customers would tell me: "You sure are the apple of your father's eye." Beaming, I understood what they meant. I was special to him, partly because I was the one in the family who looked like him, with shiny dark hair and intense brown eyes, with skin that tanned instead of burned. And I was his little girl—his real little girl. My older half-sisters had grey-blue eyes and pale hair and skin. They favored our mother, and perhaps their own dad, whom I had not met.

As Daddy strode through the greenhouses or across our fields, he would pause to lift me onto his shoulders, bouncing me up and down as he walked, or to balance me on top of his old steel wheelbarrow loaded high with dirt. He dipped and swayed as he trotted down the paths, while I shrieked, clutching the rusty edges of the barrow.

Every morning, Daddy and Mother hurried through their bowls of oatmeal to return to the greenhouses, leaving us girls to care for ourselves. As soon as Daddy left the table, even if I had not finished eating, I avoided Marilyn's glare, slipped out of my chair and followed him.

The early sun radiated through the panes of glass warming the greenhouse. Soon it filled with the aroma of moist soil that rose as Daddy watered the benches of growing plants. I loved this smell of wet earth, of dewy fresh growth. While he dragged the black hose along the walkways, rattling the gravel, I hopscotched in and out of the coiling loops to follow in his footsteps.

We had a pond built into one corner of the greenhouse, where I'd lean over the edge to dangle my hands into the murky water and talk with the elusive goldfish, velvety algae clinging to my arms. Sometimes, when the light shone at just the right angle, my face reflected back and I talked, not to the fish, but to this other girl, although I don't remember what I told her. Words sank below the surface.

When the snapdragons bloomed, I'd group them into little families, pinching their blossom-heads up and down to talk with each other, their stalk bodies touching one another gently. Even on winter days, during bad weather when the light coming through the glass roof turned flat and slate gray, the warmth of my surroundings seemed soft and comforting. The greenhouses nurtured me and felt more like my home than our real house.

Every morning, Mother picked a handful of chickweed growing in the damp ground beneath the benches to tuck into our yellow canary's cage. She'd murmur affectionately and whistle to Dickie Bird as she filled his cups with fresh water and seed. I never heard her talk to anyone like she talked to Dickie. His cage hung along the wall of windows that separated our floral shop from the greenhouse, his song floating into both. The customers entered the front door of our house into this room, where they could conduct their business or step down into the greenhouses to wander out among the flowers for sale.

During these sun-filled mornings, everything felt warm and safe. With Dickie Bird's song lilting through the air, I tagged happily along beside Daddy. But when everything darkened long before nightfall, the warmth of our mornings transformed into a heavy and cold silence between my parents. Then Daddy plodded through his tasks, shoulders drooping, his eyes vacant and far away. Remaining on the other side of the greenhouse, Mother slammed through her work, her jaw set with resignation. I shadowed Daddy and knew to avoid her. But sometimes, on the worst days, Mother cornered me, her eyes gleaming. "You're always spared, just because you're Daddy's own daughter; now Marilyn and Ellin are just step-children."

I believed what I was told and grew up accepting that I was the one responsible for our family's troubles. And I began to sense the ironic danger of staying close to Daddy for protection.

ᕀ ᕀ ᕀ

Our five acres, a sizeable amount of land within our small town, were at the north edge of the valley. We made our living from the soil, so even though we were inside the city limits, it was never clear whether we were a town business or a farm. We didn't seem to belong to either group, and, for a long time, I thought it was because of where we lived. We were like Marion itself: in the center of the country, claimed neither by the east nor the west.

Every morning he could get away, Daddy opened the cash drawer for a nickel and drove to town to join the town's business-men for their coffee break. One morning, when I must have been four years old, he took me with him.

The Cozy Café was filled with men, all wearing neatly-creased dress trousers and white shirts, some with ties. They sat on red stools by the counter, chatting as they drank coffee from chunky white mugs. As soon as we walked in, I realized how different my daddy looked. He toiled all day in the heat and dirt of our green-houses, and until now I hadn't given his appearance a thought. His tan work trousers were always dirty, with usually a knee poking through one of the holes, similar to the gap in his sweat-stained work-shirt that always had a button or two missing and remained half untucked. In our family, we took baths once a week, on Saturday night to prepare for church the next morning, and even though Daddy never attended church he bathed then, too. That's when he would change his clothes. Sometimes he shaved, sometimes he didn't. He seemed as unconcerned about his shabby, dirty clothes as he did his whiskery face and sour body odor of sweat. As I looked at the other men seated in that café, for the first time I sensed there was something wrong, but I couldn't understand what it was.

Two men dropped coins beside their cups and rose to leave. "Don't go just because I came!" Daddy said loudly with an anxious grin. Neither man looked at him.

With proud importance, he led me to the two vacant stools at the counter and ordered a coffee for himself and a hot chocolate for me. Swiveling to the men next to him he boomed, "So—what's new with you guys?" And farted. I flushed when I heard a snicker. Daddy didn't seem to notice. "So—what's new?" he repeated. One or two paused in their conversation to respond.

"Not much, Rendel. What's new with you?" Not waiting for his answer, they returned to discussing the high school football game the previous Friday night. I doubt Daddy attended, but now he joined in with much seriousness, his heavy black eyebrows raised as he agreed with everything said, repeating comments with authority as though they were his own. The men remained stiffly polite, mostly ignored him. As time slipped by Daddy stopped commenting. His face saddened; his eyes darkened with shadows. When we finished our drinks, we quietly slid off the stools and left.

Every morning I watched him go to the cash box for a nickel, get into his car and drive to town, and I filled partly with sadness, but mostly with a sense of shame.

Cracks in the Wall

❧

On a bright Saturday morning in March when I was three, I left the greenhouse to bounce my doll buggy down the step into the back room I shared with my two sisters, a room our parents had added so we girls could have a bedroom. Why did I leave that haven, where every day I stayed safe with my daddy? Bursting with a new sense of exhilaration and confidence, I gathered my doll from the quilt on my bed, tucked her into the buggy, and began twirling and whirling, the wheels sliding across the smooth gray cement floor. Look at me, my gyrating body shouted with every movement. See how pretty I am! Watch me dance!

Marilyn's job that morning was to mop our floor. She put the pail of water on the kitchen burner to heat, forgetting about it until the galvanized steel pail overheated. She found it bubbling and splashing onto the stove. I didn't hear her come into our room gripping the handle gingerly with hot pads, didn't notice when she put the pail of water in the middle of the floor to cool. She turned to the mirror on the wall, lifting her long hair, tilting her head this way and that. Startled, I saw her eyes watching me in the mirror.

I wondered what she was thinking. Her eyes in the mirror were following my dancing. Perhaps she thought I flaunted my freedom to play, while she had to mop? But that can't be; I had begun dancing before she came in. My frolicking had nothing to do with her. Perhaps she saw this as a dare? Or perhaps, after she momentarily noted my movements, she lost interest and ignored me, preoccupied with her appearance.

She brushed her long hair over and over, stretching to pull the brush the full length down her back. She ignored me. I ignored her, feeling invincible, convinced she couldn't hurt me. I turned my back and continued to sway and glide, so buoyant I imagined myself floating above the floor. Round and round the room, dancing to the music in my head, so oblivious, so filled with joy—until I thrust backward, bumping into the pail, losing my balance, and plunging into the boiling water.

As I struggled, screaming, someone strained to heft me out of the three-gallon pail, but wedged in, I couldn't budge by myself. Its 12-inch diameter formed a trap, the steel edge burning into the back of my legs. That someone pulled me free. Searing pain, a flurry of activity, shouting. Mother clutching me in the rocking chair. Daddy racing for the doctor. Ellin huddling off to the side, too frightened to cry.

Then in one moment—as in a movie when the sound suddenly stops, and things move in slow motion—everything changed. Mother clasped me tightly against herself, and for the first-and last-time in my life, I felt the tender touch of her body. This sensation seared deeper than the burns. The flurry, the shock, everything else disappeared as I flooded with awe, absorbing the softness of her breasts, the thumping of her frightened heart, her caring arms around me. While we waited for the doctor, Mother watched the skin from my waist to my knees loosen and ripple to the floor.

When Dr. Steese, the local chiropractor, examined me, she clucked her tongue. I would need a lot of help and I'd be bedfast for some time. Mother assured her she could care for me. There was no money for hospitalization.

Day after day I remained still, lapsing in and out of semiconsciousness, escaping my pain. My bedroom window opened into the greenhouse, so I could hear Mother as she worked and served the customers. She set a bell beside my pillow, that she would hear through the window, and told me to ring it when I needed her. For the first day or two she rushed when she heard the dinging to see what I wanted. Then she took the bell away. A few days later, desperate, I called out and she came, hurried and impatient. Sweat dripped from her smudged face that was lined with weariness. Frightened, I felt strangely aware of her fragility; I couldn't press her, or I might hurt her. Filled with fear, her suffering became more important than my own. I didn't call out to her again.

I dreaded the moments when her touch became necessary. If Mother was there when I had to pee, she'd roughly lift my hips onto a coffee can; I'd stiffen, trying to hold myself off its edge that felt like a knife's blade. My refusal to call her became a nightmare, if I wasn't able to wait until she came on her own. She spread newspapers on my bed and told me to go ahead and pee, that she would clean me up when she had time. But when I wasn't able to wait any longer, the urine gushing onto my raw flesh felt like searing hot liquid. Bowel movements were even worse as feces stuck and I felt like it ignited my raw flesh. The first time this happened I screamed. Mother ran to me from the greenhouse.

"I thought you really needed me," she said sharply. "You have to be quiet and wait. I'm busy with a customer. I'll come as soon as I can." I lay rigid in my waste, determined not to bother her again, wincing with the burning and the stink, the tears I also could no longer hold back flooding my cheeks.

At first, I would turn my head toward the greenhouse window, straining to overhear her conversations with customers, listening for the people to leave so Mother would be free to come:

Oh, your mums are lovely this year! I'd like two of those bronze colored ones. Try to pick the ones with the brightest color. No, not that one. The one behind it. Yes—that one. It's beautiful. On second thought put both of those back. I think I'll take two of the golden ones. They'll work better with my tablecloth. Yes, those two are perfect. Oh, you know what. Put that one back—yes, that one—and give me one of the purples—no, not that one, the one over there.

But even when the words ended, she seldom came. Eventually I stopped listening.

When she did rush in, she quickly hoisted me up, wadded the soiled newspapers and used them to rub my raw skin clean. In spite of myself, I'd cry out. She'd say sternly: "Hold still!" But then she'd pause, softening. "I'll finish this when I have more time." She'd spread fresh newspapers under me, leaving the feces stuck on my skin, and stride out.

Tears slid down my neck as I sank into the relentless pain and nightmare. Although I needed attention, I didn't want her to return. I resented the harsh washcloth and bowl of cold water. Even though she told me she would be careful, her work-roughened hands felt like sandpaper as she scrubbed me.

During those weeks of healing, I don't remember anyone coming into my room, except Mother and Dr. Steese. My stepsisters had been moved into our living area a few feet away, where they slept on the floor between the couch and the kitchen table. They never peeked in to see me. I looked down at my burns, now patchy with yellow ooze. Maybe no one wanted to look at me. I heard customers talking with Mother as they walked by, seemingly unaware that I was lying so near on the other side of the window. Whenever they had seen me playing in the greenhouses, they always spoke to me; now no one called through to say hello.

I wished Daddy would take his radio from the shelf above the potting bench and put it beside my bed. No one sat down to talk or read a story—but then, no one ever talked to each other or read stories in our home. Daddy never came to see me. Did he not want to see my burns or my pain? Yet he could have talked with me through the window without looking at me.

On the day I was burned, I have no memory of anything after the doctor left. Did Dr. Steese give me medication that made me forget? But as a chiropractor, she couldn't prescribe medications. I must have blocked out what happened around me, unable to cope with anything more, slipping off into shock. But in my fog, from far away, I heard Marilyn's strangled sobs, Daddy savagely beating her. Mother had told me Daddy's violence against my sisters was my fault. Although I never understood this, over the next days I did realize that I must have done something really bad for this to have happened to Marilyn. And I had no longer been spared. Finally, I was getting what Mother repeatedly had told me I deserved.

As days went by, to lessen my misery I developed a game to pass the time. There was a crack in the wall beside my bed that I visually traced as it climbed, turned onto the ceiling, then split into two directions. One of those cracks zigzagged toward the opposite wall; the other inched toward the doorframe but got stuck at the light fixture. I imagined these cracks as little paths. Every morning I followed them, but in spite of my willing them to move, they never lengthened to reach the door. Even in my imagination, I couldn't find a way to escape.

One afternoon, when Mother arrived to change my soiled newspaper, she stooped to look closer. "Oh my gosh!" she exclaimed, then ran out of the room and returned with one of her quart-glass canning jars. Carefully, with a large spoon, she lifted something and dropped it into the jar. "Look at this," she told me, excited. A huge worm writhed upwards against the glass.

When Dr. Steese arrived, with a triumphant gesture Mother handed her the jar. The doctor's eyes widened as she looked at it. "It's a roundworm," Dr. Steese said. "A common worm, but this one is huge. Children mostly get them from playing in dirt and mud and then putting their fingers in their mouths." She and Mother agreed my playing in the greenhouse was where I must have gotten it.

As they talked, neither of them spoke to or even looked at me lying naked on the bed. This confirmed that I was not only bad but disgusting. My skin oozed yellow, bloody pus. I stank. And now I learned, as did others, that a horrifying worm had been crawling inside me. I turned my head away and stared at the wall, wanting to escape through that enticing, yet impossible path.

Together, Mother and Dr. Steese took the worm from the jar and slit it open. Both recoiled. "Look!" the doctor exclaimed. "Thousands of them. She's lucky she passed that when she did." What exactly was that? I didn't understand they were staring at eggs, but instead believed she and Mother were looking at thousands of baby worms. I imagined they were crawling throughout my body. Even my scalp and unwashed hair seemed to writhe. My burns were beginning to heal, and I squirmed with the itching, convinced it was created by the worms that kept escaping in my feces, worms now creeping along the walls and cracks of my body to burrow into my scabs.

Weeds and Blossoms

By mid-summer my burns had healed sufficiently that I could leave our house. I returned to the greenhouse, but my months in bed left me feeling even more vulnerable and scared, unsafe now even with Daddy. One morning, while my parents were busy with customers, I slipped out the front door.

For the first time, I crossed the street. I walked along the sidewalk and studied each house, stopping at the last one on our block. It was neat and white, with emerald green shutters and a swing on the porch painted green to match. I knocked on the door.

A slender, wiry woman opened it. A frown furrowed the middle of her forehead. She wiped her hands on her faded blue apron that covered a drab navy housedress and pushed up her wire-rimmed glasses from where they had slipped down her nose. White hair, tightly curled, framed her thin face.

"Well?" she said, without warmth. We studied each other. "Did you want something?" I remained silent. "Did you come just to stand there, to say hello?" I stubbed my sandal against her doormat, nodding. Silence. She put down her dust cloth, and came out on the porch, carefully closing her door.

"Well, would you like to swing with me for a little while?"

I nodded and gingerly inched beside her onto her green wooden swing, feeling the scar tissue on my legs stretch. She pushed us back and forth with her foot. Her name was Mrs. Hazlet, she said, and asked for mine, commenting on what a pretty name I had. After more moments of silence, she stopped the swing and told me she had to return to her work. "Thank you for coming to visit," she told me before fleeing inside and shutting her door, leaving me on her porch.

The next morning, she opened her door to find me there again. Her lips tightened into a thin smile. She sighed and leaned her broom against the wall. We sat on the swing again. She asked me why I wanted to visit her, and I said that her house looked friendly. I had wanted to know who lived in it.

The following day when I knocked, she invited me inside. The light was dim, all the shades pulled down to keep out the heat. It smelled like the powder we used to scour our tub. She sat on a stiff, brown sofa and patted the space beside her. I climbed up, wincing as its bristly surface scratched my tender legs. She told me she was a religious woman and belonged to the Seventh Day Adventist church. "I prayed about you, dear, and God has laid you on my heart." Her lips curved a bit higher with satisfaction.

She explained that every morning she would read me a story from a book I'd never seen: *Bible Stories for Children.* Did I like lemon drops? She looked pleased when I exclaimed *yes!* She brought a pink bowl from her buffet filled with a small mound of those sugarcoated sweets. "Well, I bought these just for you," she said. "You can have one each time you come, as long as you sit quietly and listen to the story."

I nodded enthusiastically. I didn't understand about God laying me on her heart. She was a tiny thin woman and if God laid me across her chest, wouldn't I hurt her? I did understand that she wanted me to continue to come, and I would get a lemon drop every day. But most important, if I was quiet, she would read to me.

Each morning I arrived on Mrs. Hazlet's doorstep. She expected me now and smiled, puffing up with purpose, stepping briskly as she went for the book of stories and the candy dish. We settled onto the couch. I took my lemon drop and remained very still. No one had ever read to me. Sucking the sugar off the outside of the drop, I held it on my tongue to melt it slowly, feeling the stickiness slip down my throat, doing my best to make each drop last the length of the story. I always eyed the full dish of candies, wishing she would let me have two, but she never did. I hoped she had lots of stories.

I loved the one about baby Moses. When his mother didn't want him, she put him in a basket and floated him down the river to a woman who didn't have a baby, a woman who loved and took care of him. I studied the illustration of her hugging baby Moses and wondered if he could feel the warmth of her thumping heart?

But the story I asked Mrs. Hazlet to repeat was the one about the lost lamb. A shepherd named Jesus was tending a flock of sheep grazing on a hillside when he realized one of his lambs was missing. He went to search for her. I decided it was a girl lamb, who must have run away because a mean sister sheep in the flock was scaring her. But she wandered too far and tumbled down the side of the hill, probably scraping her lamb knee. I warmed with joy when Jesus found her. He braced himself with his staff to climb along the dangerous, steep rocks, and, reaching down, gently lifted the frightened lamb into his strong arms. I imagined he stopped other sheep from being so mean and let the little lamb stay close to him where she would stay safe.

Each day when Mrs. Hazlet finished the story, she placed the candy jar back on her buffet and ushered me to the door, giving me a slight push, explaining she had to get back to her cleaning. I always hoped the story would be a long one, but when I noticed her sitting straighter, her voice rising and speeding up, I knew we were nearing the end. Soon I found myself back on the sidewalk.

The day came when she read the last story in the book. Closing it, she laid it on the coffee table and told me she had fulfilled her promise to God. I wasn't to come anymore. Her smile tight again, she gave me an extra lemon drop. Patting my arm awkwardly, she said: "Always remember that God loves you." With her hand tightening on my arm, she walked me out the door.

I returned the next day. She was backing her car out of the driveway and, without looking at me, waved as she drove down the street. I understood. I wouldn't return again.

Instead of going home, I stopped at the large, two-storied yellow house on the other side of our property. I climbed the five wooden steps onto the porch and knocked on the door, a piece of peeling gray paint falling with my touch. Even before the elderly woman opened the door, a mouthwatering aroma greeted me. When she smiled and invited me in, I didn't hesitate.

"You knew just when to come visit me," she chortled. "I'm set to lift my bread out of that oven right now." She didn't appear to think it strange to see me and didn't even ask my name.

A starched white apron covered the front of her limp, dark blue cotton dress. Gray frizzled hair streaked with black framed a face dominated by penetrating dark eyes. Whenever she smiled, crow's feet crinkled around those dancing eyes. I followed her into the kitchen, her red felt slippers flapping against the wooden floor. Wrapping her hands around a towel, she took three pans of brown loaves out of the oven and dumped them onto cooling racks. She dropped the towel onto the table and smiled at me, wiping strands of hair away from her glistening face.

"Cobb can't stand that soft white rubbish from the store," she confided. "I bake his bread once a week, putting in all the rich goodness our sweet Lord intended us to eat." She slid the black pans into the sink already stacked with baking items and breakfast dishes. While she filled the sink with hot soapy water, she told me her name was Lizzie, and that she came every day to take care of Cobb, the old bachelor who lived here alone. She had been doing this for years, she explained, an old spinster woman herself who lived with her unmarried brother, Al, the town barber. He began barbering in that shop when he was fourteen and now owned it, she said proudly. (She couldn't know he would continue operating that shop until he sold it after seventy-three years.)

"Does your mama know you're here?" Lizzie asked. When I quickly nodded, staring at the floor, she said nothing. "Do you help your mama bake bread?" I shook my head. I didn't tell her my mother never even wanted me in the kitchen. She was seldom there herself, and then always in a rush, and the room was so tiny I would just have been underfoot. I had never smelled baked bread before. I thought it the most wonderful aroma in the whole world and eyed it hungrily. She nodded, smiling. "We'll need to let it cool, but it won't be long, and I'll cut us a big slice."

She pulled a wooden stool over beside her worktable. When she lifted me up, I ignored the twinge on my thigh, only feeling the gentleness of her strong, brown arms. She looked down into my face and gave me a squeeze, releasing a scent of talcum powder mingled with the sweat darkening her dress under her arms. She poured two glasses of milk from the metal can in the refrigerator, cut two large slices from one of the loaves, placing them on saucers, and slathered each slice with butter that melted quickly, dripping over the crusty sides. Sitting on a stool beside me, she folded her hands and closed her eyes. I gaped at her, but quickly folded my hands like hers, though I didn't close my eyes. I watched her pink lips speak. "Thank you, sweet Jesus, for giving us this food to eat, and thank you for bringing my new friend to share it with me today." I quickly shut my eyes when she announced *Amen*.

Every morning possible, I ran down the sidewalk to knock on Lizzie's door. Beaming, she opened it wide and let me help her with whatever she was baking that day. Wednesdays were oatmeal cookie day. Those cookies bulged with fat raisins and black walnuts harvested from the trees bordering the length of our street. Gingersnaps were on Monday. Lizzie and I sat side by side dipping warm cookies into our milk, giggling whenever it drizzled down our chins. Fridays were my favorite days, however, when the aroma of bread baking met me as I climbed her steps.

After she carried our dishes to the sink, she returned to her work, but unlike Mrs. Hazlet she welcomed my company. I sat on my stool while she ironed Cobb's pale blue cotton shirts, alternating her two flat irons kept hot on the black iron stove. Sweat would roll down the sides of her face and drip off her chin. "I don't need bother dampening these shirts 'fore I start," she would laugh.

One day Lizzie led me down a hall into a sunny room to meet Cobb. His lean body stretched out on an old recliner. A blanket partially covered the holes in the chair's fabric, holes with stuffing popping out. A bony big toe stuck through the end of each of his slippers. His grizzled face was deeply tanned, surrounded by unruly tufts of white hair. Sucking on a pipe between his teeth, he also worked a wad of tobacco in his cheek, seemingly unconcerned that its juice dribbled out, catching in his white stubble.

"So, you're the little girl who likes to visit Lizzie," he barked, his piercing dark eyes looking at me intently. He took a deep suck on his pipe, coughed, and turned to spit into a spattered brass bowl on the floor beside his chair. "She tells me you're a well-behaved little girl. That true?" I stared at him, tongue-tied. "You can play in my field next door any time you want, you hear?" he announced. "You take one of your little friends and gallop up and down there all you want. You like that idea?" He coughed, turned and spit into the bowl. "When you get a little older, perhaps I'll bring in one of my ponies from the farm for you to ride."

A pony? I brightened, forgetting my shyness.

"Well, that got your attention," he guffawed. "You remember what I'm saying; I won't forget." He turned, a stream of brown juice missing the bowl. "You go on now, get one of Lizzie's cookies." He nodded, curtly dismissing me, but smiled as he reached for the rumpled newspaper beside his chair.

"He likes you," Lizzie said when we were back in the kitchen. "And he'll do what he says, you wait and see. He gave a pony to Virginia to play with, the girl who lives next door to his farm." Lizzie gathered the dirty dishes and put them in her sink of soapy water. "He doesn't go there much anymore, but he still keeps a few ponies and some cows. Every other morning one of his men brings the can of fresh milk and talks over with Cobb how his fields of wheat and corn are growing. He oversees the men who take care of the farm and Cobb is good to them." She handed me a dishtowel and I wiped the dishes.

A pony. That I could keep right here in Cobb's field beside my house. Heady with excitement, I wondered how old I had to be before he would bring one. Lizzie watched me, her crow's feet crinkling. We finished the dishes. She poured our milk and put two cookies on a plate in front of me. I loved Lizzie and knew she liked me, too. I remembered that the woman who found Moses floating on the river had dark skin. I wondered if Lizzie wished she had a little girl, and if she'd mind if her skin was light.

When Daddy needed his hair trimmed, sometimes I went with him to Al's Barbershop—though everyone called him Mr. Holder, never Al. I never saw Mr. Holder look wilted, regardless of how hot the day. An oscillating fan on a high shelf twisted back and forth stirring the air. He wore a starched white shirt with a bow tie, and his black trousers remained sharply creased. He maintained a warm and friendly politeness that put people at ease, while standing erect behind his barber chair as he worked. No one seemed to notice or care that, aside from old Mr. King, who drove his horse wagon through alleys collecting trash, Mr. Holder was the only black man in town, though everyone, including the blacks themselves, at that time called them "colored." Local men dropped by to sit and talk, even when not getting their hair cut. His shop was a favorite gathering place, where the men laughed easily.

I imagined what the house looked like where Al and Lizzie lived. Clean and neat, it would be filled with the aroma of cookies and bread baking and quiet in a peaceful way, not from people being afraid. They were gentle people. At night before they ate their supper, they bowed their heads to thank their sweet Jesus. I didn't know where they lived but longed for Lizzie to invite me to visit them. She never did, and I remained too shy to ask. When she took off her apron, pulled on her wide-brimmed red straw hat with its large yellow flowers, and picked up her black pocketbook, we'd walk together down the wooden steps of Cobb's porch and say good night at the sidewalk. Lizzie walked one way, toward town, while I walked in the opposite direction, to my own home.

Sometimes, Mother scolded me if I hung around the greenhouse too much, telling me not to be a nuisance. The customers didn't seem to mind; they smiled and talked with me. I didn't understand why Mother seemed bothered, but I remembered her words and didn't want to risk being a nuisance with Lizzie. Some days I began visiting other houses on our street.

The Atterberrys lived on the other side of us. They had no children and never answered the door when I knocked. Mrs. Atterberry pulled aside the curtain to peek out once, then quickly closed it. I stopped knocking, but once when I saw them working in their large vegetable garden I walked around to sit on the grass and watch. She gave me a quick little smile as she knelt beside a row of peas or green beans, nudging her basket ahead of her with her knee as she picked. She seldom spoke; her husband never said hello, never even looked up from his hoeing. I understood they didn't want me there. Now I understood what it felt like to be a nuisance. I didn't return.

The Griggs lived in the large white house across the street. Mrs. Griggs, a heavy-set woman with stringy black hair, never seemed bothered by my being there—a quiet girl among her noisy boys. She was always working. Stirring a large pot at her stove, she'd pause to wipe her face on her grease-splattered apron, nodding that we could have a graham cracker from the open box on her cluttered table. She lugged her baskets, heavy with wet sheets and denim overalls, up from their basement to the backyard, where she would let me hold the clothespin basket and hand the pins to her. I wanted to help her hang the clothes but couldn't reach the line above my head. Clicking the pins, I pretended they were talking animals, and flushed with pleasure when she laughed. I loved how she talked and laughed easily with all of us kids.

Indoors, winding stairs led to the second floor, where her boys occupied the two large bedrooms. I loved clattering up and down the wooden steps (our house was all on one level). The scattered mess of unmade beds, clothes tossed on the floor, a few toys here and there seemed a paradise to me. Lawrence, who was my age, shared his wooden cars and trucks. We sped them around mounds of dirty clothes, up bedposts and across mountains of heaped blankets before crashing off cliffs. Sometimes I wore the high-top boots of Otis, his oldest brother, raising my feet high to clump around on their bare wooden floors.

I wanted to sleep snuggled among the rumpled quilts on the wide beds that had room for everyone. But as evening approached, even though I hoped Mrs. Griggs would forget me, she'd call up the stairs: "It's suppertime, dear. Time for you to go home." I'd look longingly at their family gathering around their table, as I passed through the kitchen and out the door to sit on the porch steps, hoping she would come back out and invite me to stay for supper, but it never happened. Their table was already crowded. Reluctantly, I crossed the street to my own house. No one at home seemed to even have noticed my having been gone, or that I had now returned.

❧ ❧ ❧

My exploration of my neighborhood continued that summer. Some days I didn't knock on any door but would walk up and down the sidewalk, choosing a house that looked inviting. From the sidewalk, I tried to peer through the windows. Surely there were people who lived differently than we did. I wanted to know what they did inside. But I never could see past the curtains. Sometimes I sat beneath a tree and with a stick drew pictures in the dirt, creating a house with a family living there. I made up stories of my make-believe family, where everyone was always kind to each other. The parents would enjoy listening to their kids, and smile at them, even laugh. Everyone talked together as they ate around their table, and after supper they might play Dominoes or Monopoly, or lie around on the floor listening while the mother read books out loud to them all. No one yelled. No one hit. The kids could laugh without being afraid.

One day I ventured beyond where the sidewalk ended, walking in the street around the bend. There the brick changed to gravel, marking the end of town. A large white farmhouse stood beyond an alfalfa field, surrounded by giant oak trees. Pots of pink and white petunias bloomed on their front porch. The name "Pope" was painted on the gray mailbox. I climbed the steps and knocked on their door.

A girl opened it. She looked near my age, though taller and thinner, with lighter brown hair and eyes. We stood looking at one another, curious. "Did you come to visit me?" When I nodded, she smiled and opened the door, inviting me in. "I'm Kathryn," she said, "I'm five." I told her my name, and that I was four.

Kathryn led me to their kitchen to meet her mother. Mrs. Pope was a tall, large-boned yet thin woman, graying hair pulled back into a bun from her plain face. She wore a faded apron made from a patterned flour sack over her simple cotton dress. Her bustling energy filled the kitchen as she washed dishes, stirred a large pot of bubbling soup, and stooped to peek into the oven while greeting me with a warm smile. A delicious aroma wafted throughout the room. Six loaves of bread stood cooling on the wooden kitchen table, and now she pulled two cherry pies from the oven, their red juices oozing through their top crusts.

Mrs. Pope prompted Kathryn to offer me a seat and bring three plates from the cabinet. She placed one of the loaves on a wooden board, scarred with knife marks, and cut thick slices for each of us. I stared as she stopped her work to sit, eat, and talk with us, as though this was the most important thing she had to do. Kathryn brought a pot of butter from their refrigerator, bragging that just that morning she had churned it herself, and that she had helped her mother make the jar of peach jam last summer from fruit they picked in their orchard. Mrs. Pope asked me about myself, and while I talked, she looked at me, listening. By the time we finished our bread and jam, I knew Kathryn was my new friend and that I was welcome in this home. When I left, both Kathryn and her mother walked me to the door and invited me to come back, which I did often that summer. I still went first to say good morning to Lizzie every day, my love for her never diminishing, and sometimes stopped at the Griggs house. But at Kathryn's, I became part of a family at last.

Kathryn was responsible for chores every day and let me help her. First, we tended the chickens. I carried the wire basket for the eggs, while she lugged the pail of feed. Closing the wobbly wooden gate behind us, we'd enter their chicken yard—five fenced acres shaded by huge walnut trees. Chickens roamed everywhere, scratching in the leaves and dirt. At my home, our few chickens lived in a small square pen enclosed by a sagging wire fence, moving at night into a tiny shed. The pen was at the end of our property, near the creek, surrounded by weeds that I knew were filled with snakes. When I had to feed the chickens, I crept through the weeds, alert for the invisible presence that slithered silently parting stalks and tossed the pail of food over the fence and fled.

With Kathryn, I imitated her and flung fistfuls of grain for the clucking hens, squealing when they brushed against me, their soft feathers tickling my bare legs. We went into the dim, feathery mustiness of the large white chicken house to gather the eggs. At first, I hesitated. It felt spooky, but Kathryn wasn't afraid. She showed me how to reach under a hen nestled in one of the hay-lined boxes. Watching the bird warily, I slipped my hand under her belly, bursting with delight each time I pulled out a warm egg. Together we carried the full wire basket between us to show her mother. Mrs. Pope checked the eggs, always praising us for doing a good job.

Their chicken yard became our favorite place to play. Some afternoons we played catch with her orange ball, hurling it back and forth over the chicken house, yelling, "Alley—Alley—Over." But our favorite pastime was raking clean long tracks for roadways, then using the leaves and debris to shape our little village, connecting all our imaginary buildings with long twisting roads over which we raced our tricycles, careening around the corners as we acted out our daily routines. I became engrossed in this play, spending most of my time creating a house for my imagined family.

Fetching water from their well was another of Kathryn's chores. Together we slid the wooden cover to the side and lowered the galvanized pail on a rope until it splashed. Shaking the rope to make the pail tip into the water, we felt it grow heavy. Together we hauled it up and carried it into the kitchen, placing it on the end of the cabinet. Kathryn hung a tin dipper on the side of the pail. She ladled this into the water and showed me how she tilted it to her mouth and drank deeply. She refilled it and handed it to me. The cold edge of the tin and the sweetness of the cool water surprised me. Her mother smiled and said they treasured their pure water, and never drank the hard city water filled with chemicals.

At our house, the water tasted bitter. White crust edged and clogged our faucets. I dreaded every Saturday night, the time when Mother washed my hair. She hated this routine as much as I did, but my hair had to be clean for Sunday school the next morning. While hamburger and sliced potatoes sizzled in the frying pan, she hurried me onto the kitchen cabinet, where I stretched out and hung my head backwards over the sink. I pressed the dishcloth to my eyes, while Mother's calloused hands scrubbed through my long hair. When she finished, she poured vinegar over my hair to soften the harsh water. In her haste, she often poured it over my entire head, the vinegar soaking through the dishcloth into my eyes, nose and mouth even though I squeezed them shut and pressed the dishcloth hard. I squirmed and choked but lay still and swallowed it when she snapped at me.

One night during supper Daddy erupted at Marilyn, his face turning purplish-red as he grabbed the tin milk pitcher and waved it round and round like a lariat, milk spraying through the air before he slung it at her. The pitcher slammed into her face. Blood spurted from her nose. Milk splattered all of us. We sat rigid and silent, dripping. Marilyn stifled her sobs and pinched her nose, trying to stop the blood.

"Oh Rendel," Mother cried. "Now I'll have to wash Roberta's hair all over again."

ɞ ɞ ɞ

When we felt sure Kathryn's mother was occupied elsewhere in the house, sometimes Kathryn and I would pull open the flour bin in the kitchen cabinet to drag our fingers through the white mass. I had never played in a large mound of flour before, and soon realized it was much more fun than a sand pile. We took turns with spoons from the drawer in their kitchen table, one of us using a soupspoon to sculpt large objects, while the other used a teaspoon to shape smaller designs. Leaning over the front of the bin, Kathryn and I alternated thumbs with our fingers or spoons to shape our buildings and animals, often crossing over each other's hands as we worked, the same way we played "Chopsticks" side-by-side at her piano.

After a time, Kathryn would become uneasy, reminding me her mother didn't like her playing in the baking flour. I hesitated. Neither of us wanted to disobey her mother, yet it was so much fun we kept going, hoping she wouldn't find out. Whenever we heard footsteps, we hurriedly smoothed out the flour and closed the bin, wiping the spoons on our clothes before tossing them back into the drawer. One day we didn't hear her mother before she walked in. I froze, certain she would be angry and send me home. She stood looking at us quietly, then told Kathryn we were not to play in the flour, and she left the room. We looked at each other, then closed the bin and never played in it again.

Even though Kathryn and I longed to romp around on the hay in their barn's loft, we never did play in their barn. Her father told us there were too many risks for little girls. He didn't want either of us to get hurt. But I knew better; he just didn't want us to mess up his barn. Mr. Pope's appearance was similar to my daddy's—both were short and stocky, had soft dark brown eyes, and were perpetually tanned from working outdoors all year. They each grew bald in an identical way: hair disappearing on top, leaving a dark and narrow horseshoe fringe around the sides. I felt kindness in Mr. Pope's quiet manner, just as I felt with my Daddy when we worked alone together in the greenhouse. Yet I knew how quickly this could change. It was just a matter of time before I would see Mr. Pope erupt too. I remained vigilant.

We often ran to watch him return from the fields at the end of the day. I was in awe of his giant workhorses and helped Kathryn pour oats into their feeding buckets in preparation for their arrival. We stood at a distance as his weary team pulled the rumbling wooden wagon into the barnyard. Mr. Pope dropped the reins and climbed down. After closing the gate, he disconnected the harness and patted the horses' flanks signaling for them to wander over and drink from the water tank. He unhooked the chute connected to the windmill, channeling water into the tank for the horses—sweet clear water from the same source as the water that Kathryn and I pulled from their family well.

On Sunday nights, and often on Wednesdays, I walked with the Pope family to the Baptist Church for evening services. I sat beside Kathryn on the long pew with her family. We sang a lot, the pipe organ soaring above our voices. Kathryn's and my favorite hymn was "What a Friend We Have in Jesus." We held the black hymnal together and sang at the top of our voices, glancing at each other knowingly: we had a friend in each other, too.

As often as I could, I lingered at Kathryn's until they invited me for supper. The Popes must have called my parents, though I'm not sure and never saw them phone. My parents never seemed concerned when I didn't come home. I simply stayed at the Popes'. Kathryn's family warmly embraced me into their family circle, designating a chair just for me at their large round oak table, between Mr. Pope and Kathryn's older sister. Kathryn sat between her mother and older brother. We bowed our heads while someone thanked God for our food and our rich blessings. Everyone ate slowly, talked, and even laughed. The first-time laughter burst out I stiffened and stopped chewing. In our house laughing was dangerous. It made Daddy uncomfortable, often triggering him to erupt angrily. I watched Mr. Pope warily, and even though I gradually relaxed a little, I remained on edge.

One evening during supper, everyone grew increasingly quiet. Something was wrong. Uneasily, I watched Kathryn, never having seen her behave this way. She was irritable, sassed her parents and made sullen retorts if anyone tried to speak to her. Her father glanced at her mother. She nodded and scooted back her chair. I lay down my fork. Her mother touched Kathryn's shoulder. Without a word, she rose and they both left the room. I heard the kitchen door leading to the back porch open, then close.

Turning cold, I began to shake, listening for the blows, for Kathryn's screams. The rest of the family returned to comfortably talking and finishing their supper. I stared at my plate, frozen, unable to eat. When Kathryn and her mother returned, they slid into their chairs and continued their meal, entering the conversation as though nothing had happened. Kathryn, now relaxed and friendly, had no tear stains on her cheeks.

I remained rigid and confused, my stomach in spasms, so scared I couldn't lift my fork. Her mother looked at me. "Everything's all right, Roberta," she said tenderly. "Don't let your supper get cold." Kathryn smiled at me. Her father, listening to his son relate a funny incident, chuckled, then turned to his wife. "That plum cobbler sure smells good from the kitchen, Mother. Isn't it time we get to taste it?" Everyone laughed. I picked up my fork and finished my food.

Kathryn's father walked me home through the darkness later that evening. Neither of us talked. Though I had anticipated anger, I had never felt any tension in their home. After that night, I no longer remained on guard around Mr. Pope. And I never again walked through our neighborhood, peering into strangers' houses, searching.

School Days

~

That September, the pealing of the bell rang across our valley on the Tuesday after Labor Day, signaling the first day of school. All the neighborhood kids set out for the Bown-Corby elementary school house, a small red brick building dedicated to the two women who had been the first teachers in our small community.

I sat on my green tricycle watching everyone walk past on the other side of the street, seething with jealous resentment. I realized that after playing at Kathryn's house all summer, our lives were going in separate directions. She waved from the other side of the street, wearing a new dress, walking with other kids—tall with new importance. Already five by September, Kathryn could start first grade. I wouldn't be five until my birthday in late October, so I had to wait until the following year. I watched her disappear down the sidewalk. Things would be different now. She was going to school, joining with new friends; I was the only one left behind, the youngest in the neighborhood.

I rammed my tricycle wheel over and over against the black walnuts littering the sidewalk, shattering the bright green hulls, watching the dark brown juices squish onto the cement. Kathryn would learn how to read. I wanted to learn how to read.

In Sunday school, I sat with the other children on red wooden chairs in a semicircle, listening to the stories Miss Jewell read to us. They were about boys and girls and their families far away in the Holy Land. Some stories were the same ones Mrs. Hazlet had read to me. I never wanted story hour to end.

The week before school started, Kathryn showed me her new navy-blue school bag, filled with all the things she and her mother bought at Rexall Drug Store: two #2 yellow pencils; a box of crayons—all eight colors including not only the orange and purple but the white and black; a box of chalk sticks; a 12-inch ruler; a large red Indian Chief tablet; and a jar of white paste. She took off the lid so I could sniff how good it smelled, but she yelled and grabbed it back when I stuck my finger in to taste it. The treasure in her bag, though, was the book. The yellow and blue cover showed a boy and girl throwing a red ball with their dog. Kathryn promised she would read it to me as soon as she learned the words, but I didn't want to listen to her. I pouted, wanting my own yellow and blue book.

The school bell rang again. Now 9:00 a.m., school had begun. Stillness settled around me. I roared my tricycle up and down our sidewalk, crushing every walnut in my path. Then I slid off and began walking.

Tugging the heavy school door open, I slipped into a sun-filled entryway. A flight of stairs went upstairs, and another went down. The muffled silence smelled strange—an oily cleanness. Upstairs along a hallway there were four doors, the top half of each one was a glass window. I peeked through the first and saw only big kids. I moved to the next door. Finally, through the last window, I saw Kathryn.

There were five rows of wooden desks in which kids sat facing the front of the room, listening to a young woman. Everything glowed with the sunlight streaming through the south wall of windows. Philodendron crept along the windowsills, one winding around a glass bowl holding two orange and white goldfish. Large blackboards, with colorful posters hanging above them, filled the entire front wall and half of the side wall.

Breathing faster, my heart pounding, I opened the door and walked in. Everyone turned to stare. The teacher stopped talking. Startled, Kathryn mouthed a message to me that I couldn't understand. The teacher noticed. "Do you know who this is?" she asked. Kathryn nodded, flushed, and lowered her eyes. "Do you need Kathryn?" the teacher asked me. I didn't answer, looking around the room for an empty desk.

The teacher leaned over to speak with Kathryn. Together they approached me. Kathryn looked uncomfortable. Drawing closer she hissed: "Go home. You're going to get me in trouble." I didn't want to make trouble for her, but I had to stay.

The teacher's warm blue eyes studied me, her painted-pink lips friendly. Feeling less confident now but desperate, I looked into her face and began babbling how I wanted to learn how to read and have a blue and yellow book of my own and I was almost five and wouldn't cause any trouble and please could I stay? She leaned down, her face level with mine, and said that she would love to teach me how to read, but I was too young and had to go home. With a smile, but a gentle, firm hand she guided me into the hallway. "I'll look forward to having you here next year," she said kindly, and closed the door.

Stretching on tiptoe, I looked through the window, watching the teacher return to the front of the room. Kathryn glared, motioning me to go away. I slid to the floor. The gray and white granite of the floor gleamed in the light from the windows above the stairwell. Muffled voices whispered through the door. I strained to hear, but when I couldn't understand what they were saying, I wrapped my arms around my knees and buried my head.

Sensing a presence, I opened my eyes. In front of my feet was a wide, white dust mop and beyond, the cuffs of gray work trousers drooping over scuffed black shoes. Looking up, I met a pair of grey-blue eyes behind steel-rimmed glasses. Silver hair curled around the man's tanned face. He leaned against his mop handle and studied me. Then he pulled a silver watch out of a tiny front pocket in his trousers, a watch connected to his belt loop by a silver chain. He popped open the cover. "Why, it's time for recess," he said. "How would you like to ring the bell?" He reached a warm calloused hand into mine and helped me to my feet.

Attached to the side of the school building was a small alcove where the silver metal bell hung from a beam inside the slanted roof. Steps down led to the door into the maintenance room. A knotted rope dangled down from the bell, too high for me to reach. He lifted me up, one of his arms holding me around my waist, his other reaching over my head to grasp the rope. He showed me where to grab one of the knots, then together we pulled, up and down, up and down, four times, his arm stretching, each pull pressing my body into his muscled chest: DING-dong... DING-dong... DING-dong... DING-dong. He set me down. "Now watch," he chuckled.

Within moments, the doors flew open and children ran out onto the playground, shouting and racing, trying to grab a space on the merry-go-round or to claim one of the swings. Several glanced at me curiously. I pulled myself as tall as I could to stand beside my new friend. Together we leaned against the brick wall, silently watching. After fifteen minutes, he said: "Okay, I need some help here. Just one pull this time."

He lifted me up so we could tug the rope together. The children hurried to form two straight lines by the door. The principal, Miss Thompson, stood quietly waiting for everyone to settle down, then opened the door and led them into the building.

"Well, I'd better get back to work." He looked down at me. "You're a spunky one you are." He thought for some moments. "I'm glad you came to visit me. I get pretty tired having to ring that bell all by myself. Maybe you'll want to come help me again? If you do, come to this door and knock. I'm usually here, but if I'm not, sit down on the step and wait for me. I'm never far away."

My tricycle waited on the sidewalk just where I'd left it. I jumped onto the seat and began peddling very fast, speeding toward the next September.

℘ ℘ ℘

Daddy backed his chair away from the supper table. "You girls take care of Roberta. Mother and I are going to the movies."

Did he mean it? Since my burns, he'd never left me alone with Marilyn. I stood in the middle of the kitchen in disbelief and watched them go, heard the garage door open, then shut.

"Now we've got her!" Marilyn shrieked.

She leaped forward, pulled the kitchen stool into the middle of the room, and hefted me up. She grinned at Ellin, who looked afraid and hung back. Marilyn opened a drawer and pulled out the butcher knife Mother kept in the frame of the washhouse during the summer months. The curved blade gleamed. I remembered the headless chicken. My body grew heavy.

Marilyn stood in front of me, her high laugh piercing. I wanted to cover my ears, but I couldn't lift my hands. Looking worried, Ellin never spoke and stayed removed, behind Marilyn.

Marilyn held the knife in front of my face. "You're to do exactly what I tell you, or you know what's going to happen." I clutched the edge of the stool. "Now—I want to see you laugh," Marilyn said. "Laugh! And make it loud."

A coughing sound rasped from my mouth. She stopped. Leaning closer, face flushed, and narrowing her eyes, she lowered her voice. "I told you to laugh, and you'd better laugh." She placed the knife's edge against my throat.

I laughed.

"Why are you laughing? I want you to cry!" She pressed the knife harder. "You'd better start crying—and I want to see real tears."

Scrunching up my face, I tried to force tears from my eyes. She peered closely at me, frowning, until a few drops rolled down my cheeks. I trembled, my teeth chattering.

Marilyn's shrill voice rose. "What? Are you crying? I told you to laugh." She grinned back at Ellin who had been inching away. But now, caught in Marilyn's glare, she moved back beside her.

I forced a laugh through my rigid lips.

"Why are you laughing? I want to see tears. Real tears. Now!"

With each command, the knife pressed painfully into my skin. I cringed, whimpering. Marilyn leaned into my face, so close I smelled her sour breath, felt droplets of spit as she shouted. I strained to obey—laughing, then crying, then laughing, then crying, real tears.

Their voices dimmed. A cottony softness enveloped me as I slipped into a place deep within myself, a cushioned, silent chamber. Inside my cocoon, I no longer heard Marilyn's commands or felt the knife against my throat. I didn't feel or hear anything. Safe in my private space, I realized I had discovered a new way to escape.

After two and a half hours, the garage door opened, though no one heard it. Daddy and Mother walked into the room. They appeared far away, Daddy's voice sputtering faintly across the distance. "What the …?" His face flushed crimson.

Marilyn and Ellin froze.

Daddy charged after Marilyn. She dropped the knife and raced into the back bedroom we girls shared. I didn't see or hear anything else. Everything turned black as I slithered off the stool and hit the floor. I awoke on my bed, still in my clothes, the house dark and quiet, except for Marilyn's muffled sobs. I slipped under my quilt and covered my head.

Daddy and Mother never left us alone again. But one night, after all the lights were out, Marilyn crept across the room and whispered: "I haven't forgotten. One day you're going to open the door and I'll be there. I'll get you."

Our family continued its silence, but for me everything felt heavier. No one noticed my mouth that was too exhausted to speak words. My body felt stuffed with cotton, which made everything seem remote and far away, every movement slowed. At times, I became aware someone was speaking to me, but had to blink my mind several times before I could understand the person's words. I lived apart, in a dream-like space no one else could enter.

Winter stretched into one long, cold silence. We were trapped in its icy grip, frozen people struggling through the motions of being alive.

◡ ◡ ◡

Did I walk with Kathryn to school the following September? I only remember that the first-grade classroom I had visited with so much eagerness the year before had been bright and colorful. The same room and the same teacher now were dim in hazy monotones. I sat at a desk, opened the top, placed my things inside, and waited. Kids moved and chattered around me, their voices floating from far away.

The bell rang. Miss Johnson walked to the front of the room and began talking. I listened but kept missing words. She told us to open our Red Chief tablets and draw a picture of our family. When I turned to my page and opened my box of crayons, the familiar fear returned. I disappeared.

I felt Miss Johnson's hand on my shoulder, gently shaking me. "My, you were dreaming," she said softly. "I asked you your name." I looked up at her, confused and mute. She glanced at my blank page, rubbed my stiff shoulders, then moved on down the row of desks.

I never knew when I would slip back into my cocoon. It wasn't a choice I controlled. Often when Miss Johnson explained how to do something new her words seemed jumbled. I watched those around me pick up their pencils to begin—begin what? I would flood with fear, and then... I'd be gone.

Super Heroes

ᕲ

During that first year of school, I remained closed-off and fearful, and seldom visited my neighborhood families. I reverted to staying close to Daddy in the greenhouse. Perched on a short platform he built for me, I stood beside him at the potting bench. The sun, slanting through the glass-paned roof, warmed the rows of moss-covered wooden benches filled with young plants for spring sales. During these afternoon hours, the day's accumulated warmth wrapped us in pungent humidity. The perfume of pink and lavender sweet peas, creeping along the trellis strung tautly above the benches, mingled with the fragrance from the pink and white Rubrum lilies Mother cultivated in the shaded corners. Permeating everything was the aroma of fusty, moist, fertile soil. I smelled it as soon as I unlatched the warped door and stepped inside. The scent clung to my skin long after I left.

Day after day at the potting bench, I crumbled clods of dirt between my fingers, pressing them through a crookedly framed wire screen. Daddy mixed this soil with peat moss, scooping it into wooden flats he prepared for spring seedlings. While we worked, we listened to the dusty Motorola radio on a shelf above us, following the serial episodes of my superheroes: The Lone Ranger, The Shadow, and Jack Armstrong, The All-American Boy.

I loved the Ranger's adventures, but the Shadow fascinated me. An invisible man, he began each episode warning in his deep voice: "Who knows… what evil… lurks in the hearts of men? The Shadow knows." Then he laughed that sinister laugh that made me feel shivery inside. Able to see into the hearts of bad people who couldn't see him, he stopped them before they hurt anyone. With him, only the bad people suffered; he kept innocent people safe. I doubted he would ever come to a small town in Kansas, to look into our secrets. He stayed in big cities, like New York or Los Angeles, beating up corrupt government leaders. But if he did come, I trusted he would fix the terrors I struggled to understand—that he would stop my daddy beating my sisters.

Jack Armstrong was a visible boy, ready to fight bad guys too. He showed up all over the country, even in small towns, protecting the innocent and bringing justice. I wished he would come to our home, yet if he did maybe he'd take away my daddy, the only person who protected me. Confused, I tried to figure all this out.

Over months, I saved enough Wheaties box tops to order Jack Armstrong's decoder ring. When it arrived, Daddy and I paused in our work to copy down the letters that contained the coded message for that week. Wiping the dirt off his hands onto his worn work trousers, Daddy leaned over my shoulder, his familiar smell of warm sweat settling between us, his gentle voice explaining. He watched as I twisted the ring back and forth, telling me each letter that together would reveal the secret message. I didn't grasp that the code simply reversed the alphabet: Z meant A, Y meant B, and so on. Alone, I couldn't grasp any of the codes: not the ones in the ring, not the ones in our silent house, not the ones hidden in the darkness that gripped us. Everything remained a mystery, and I depended on Daddy to help me put the letters in the right order.

Recently, I noticed my father had become increasingly quiet. I needed him to be my real live superhero, so I interpreted his silence as wise goodness. I trusted that he knew the code, so if he chose, just as he helped me decode the secret messages on my All-American Boy ring, he could help me understand the secrets our family never talked about. While I worked with him at the potting bench, I believed in our oneness with those heroic crusaders for justice.

Each day when evening approached, we left the greenhouse and returned home. Daddy lathered up his hands and arms at the kitchen sink with Lava soap, turning his bent elbows back and forth under the faucet, then slumped heavily into his chair, leaning an arm on either side of his plate, hanging his head. When Mother put the food on the table, Daddy, not shifting his position, wearily forked his food into his mouth. Mother slipped into her chair, preoccupied, probably thinking about what she needed to do in the greenhouses before she could fall into bed. My two sisters sat on the opposite side of the table from me. No one spoke. We ate silently, eyes focused on our plates.

Because I sat next to Daddy, even with my eyes lowered, I knew when things began to change, felt the heat flooding through his body, sensed the muscles in his neck begin to bulge. His eyes would be riveted on Marilyn, watching her every move, until something triggered his explosion. I never knew what it would be.

During her years of early adolescence Marilyn was a thin, shapeless, gaunt-faced girl whose brow continually furrowed. She seldom looked straight into anyone's face, and even though she tucked her stringy long brown hair behind her ears, it slipped down to hide her own face. She lived shrunk into the hopelessness of defeat. But after she turned fourteen, she rapidly began developing into a shapely, provocative young woman.

She often stood for hours primping in front of the mirror, arranging her hair into an upsweep and enlarging her mouth with red lipstick she bought from the dime store. She learned how to make her own clothes, skin-tight tops that emphasized her voluptuous breasts, and slacks snug across her hips to flare out into extra-wide bell bottoms that swayed languorously with each step as she walked. Her eyes were the only thing that betrayed her, eyes haunted with fear rather than the allure of a young siren. In spite of all her attempts, however, she remained without friends, isolated socially. Neither she nor Ellin ever went anywhere with friends.

Daddy grew increasingly bothered by her, I couldn't understand why, but it led to many of his unexpected explosions, especially during meals, one of the few times we were all close together. One night he chased Marilyn from the supper table into our bedroom, roaring like a beast. Not quite five years old, I slid from my chair to stand in the doorway and watch. Marilyn crouched in the far corner, her hands covering the top of her head trying to protect herself as he repeatedly raised our wooden softball bat high above his own head and crashed it down on hers. When he slung the bat across the room and strode past me, heat of his rage radiated from his body in waves.

"Eat that," he ordered another evening, when she took a lump of gristle from her mouth and placed it on the side of her plate. She sputtered, her eyes filling with tears. She understood if she didn't obey the table would erupt into shouts and fists.

She stared at the gristle, whimpering. "No," she whispered.

He leaped from his chair at the same moment she jumped out of her own, both of them dashing through the kitchen and out the front door. She stumbled and fell in the grass, struggling to her hands and knees, but he caught up and straddled her, pounding her back with his fists. She choked with sobs, tears mixed with bloody saliva drooling from her mouth. The rest of us huddled on the front porch, Ellin hiding behind Mother and me. A familiar spasm gripped my stomach.

"Oh Rendel," Mother wailed. "The neighbors will see."

I couldn't understand why Daddy treated my sisters so savagely, yet he was all I had, and I clung to my belief in his goodness. Alone in the comfortable silence we shared in the greenhouse he was kind and gentle. I concluded my sisters must be at fault, especially Marilyn. Why couldn't she stop doing whatever upset him? But late at night, as I listened to my sisters' sobs muffled under their blankets, I'd bury myself under my own blanket, stiff with fear and confusion.

Although I was too young to understand, on some deep level I knew my sisters were innocent. It would take many years for me to learn that families can have their secret codes, too, and what appears to be A might actually be Z.

Contagious

❧

Miss Spencer paused beside my desk, leaned over, and placed her hand on my forehead. "Oh, my goodness, Roberta— you're burning up! What are you doing here?" It was the end of November, my second year in school. I had just turned six.

I felt sick walking to school, but I often did. Even though my head hurt more than usual, it never occurred to me to tell my parents or consider staying home. No one in our house ever spoke of feeling sick. I never saw either of my parents once lie down because they weren't feeling well, or simply to rest. Once when I mentioned my head hurt, Mother set her jaw in that familiar, determined way: "Whenever I have a headache I just get to work and forget about it." We lived by our unspoken rule never to give in to or even acknowledge weakness, and that included getting ill, or even tired.

At my desk, I pressed my forehead into the tender coolness of Miss Spencer's hand. When she lifted my braids off my neck and saw red spots, she sent me to the principal's office. An epidemic of scarlet fever was spreading through our community. Miss

Thompson, the principal, told me to go home, and notified Dr. McCandless, the County Health Agent.

Dr. McCandless arrived at my house before I did. He stood on our porch arguing with my parents, explaining that the law required him to tack a large red sign beside our front door that warned in bold letters: Contagion! That created a problem. Our house was annexed by the greenhouse. We had converted our living room into the floral shop that connected the two, thus our front door became the entryway to our business. That warning would turn everyone away.

I sank down on the sidewalk, listening. They reached a compromise. Because it was required that the warning sign be posted where I would be staying, Mother decided I could stay in the apartment in our backyard, where her mother, Mabel Larson, now lived. Posted there, the warning sign would be out of the sight of customers. Mother strode ahead of Dr. McCandless along the sidewalk that circled the garage to the back of our property. I followed. Per her instructions, the doctor hammered the sign in place beside the door of the apartment.

Mabel jerked the door open, scowling. Mother hustled me past her. "Roberta's sick. She has to stay here with you for ten days. There's no other choice." Grandma stared at her open-mouthed, her face darkening. Mother didn't look at either one of us as she turned and hurried away; Dr. McCandless followed.

Grandma Larson had come to live with us the year before. Until then I had never seen her and knew only that each December I received a card saying, "Merry Christmas from Grandma Larson." She lived with her aunt in a Chicago suburb, but when the aunt died and the house was sold, Mabel phoned Mother that she had no money and nowhere to go. Even though she and

Mother never talked or saw each other (because Grandma hated my father, I heard Mother say once) Mother now told Daddy she couldn't turn her back on her mother when she was destitute. She convinced him to let her stay with us. The local carpenter attached a self-catering room (that we called the "apartment") onto the end of the washhouse that stood alone in our backyard. Mabel arrived on the Trailways bus, carrying one shabby cardboard suitcase, and moved in. That entire year after her arrival, I never knocked on her door, I never saw anyone in our family knock, and Grandma never stepped into our house.

I hung my head avoiding Grandma's eyes. She stalked across the room into the bathroom and slammed the door behind her. I stood in the center of the room, shivering. When she didn't come out, I crept over to the couch, lay down and closed my eyes, careful not to touch her blanket folded on the end.

During our ten days together, Grandma seldom spoke to me. Every night we shared the pullout couch, each clinging to a far edge. Grandma drew the only blanket around her shoulders, leaving not enough to cover me. On the first night, when I told her I felt cold, she threw the blanket at me and disappeared into the bathroom. I never asked to share it again. Shivering, I would wait until I heard her deep breathing, then lift a corner and slide in against her back.

Every morning she gave me a glass of milk with two pieces of dry burnt toast. "Eat it," she insisted, through rigid lips. "The charcoal is good for you." When I hesitated, she warned me that, if I didn't eat it, she would force me to drink my urine, which had even better purifying qualities. Every morning I grabbed the blackened toast and gobbled it down.

Grandma sat in the rocking chair crocheting, her spikes of thin, gray hair around her head quivering rhythmically with the movements of her chair. Below her silver-rimmed glasses, which slid low on her nose, the puckered frown of her mouth mirrored the tight furrowed lines in the center of her forehead. Brown cotton stockings drooped around her skinny legs, the rubber bands meant to hold them in place slipping below her knees. On the couch, I would lean over onto my side to nap, pulling my knees up against my stomach and wrapping my arms around them to keep warm. During the first days I slept often, the only times I wouldn't feel my head hurting, but even after I began to feel better, I pretended to sleep.

Some afternoons Grandma listened to people talk on her radio. I remained quiet, tracing tiny sections along the geometric pattern of the sofa with my finger, creating make-believe places and stories. Rapunzel was my favorite. Small squares in the fabric expanded taller and taller into a tower, one square squeezing into a small circle-shaped window. I imagined a face, my own, staring out from this opening and dreamed of letting down my long, dark, braided hair to escape into my daddy's arms. But even though I tried over and over to crawl over the sill of my tower window, I never made it. The witch always spied me, yanking my hair to drag me back.

In the mornings, Mother left food on the porch with a quick knock on the door, never stopping to talk. As evening approached, I sat beside the window, waiting to see Daddy on his way to feed the chickens. I hoped he would look over at me, but he always kept his head down. Whenever she heard his boots trudging by, Grandma's frown deepened, her crochet hook stabbing the colored twine, while she muttered about "that lazy bum" and how hard Mother had to work because she married him. She glowered at me. "And if you had never been born, he'd be taking better care of

Marilyn and Ellin. Now they're nothing but stepchildren." I closed my eyes, rushing back into my tower.

For a long time, Saturday morning had been the most special time of the week for me, when the radio program *Let's Pretend* broadcast. I loved to join in when they sang the opening song: "Cream of wheat is so good to eat, yes we have it every day! We sing this song 'cause it makes us strong and it makes us shout hooray!" They read a different fairy tale every week. The cast spoke the voices of the characters, and for thirty minutes each Saturday a story came alive. I blended into the magic.

During this quarantined period, when Saturday arrived, I watched the hands of the clock creep toward ten. Shaking, I asked Grandma please could I listen to her radio for half an hour? She scowled as usual but turned it on—the volume so low no one could hear it. "Would you turn it up a little bit?" I whispered.

She stalked across the room, twisted the knob up full volume, then slammed into the bathroom. I grabbed her blanket against my ears to muffle the squawking blare. When she didn't appear, I tiptoed across the floor and turned the volume down. Before I could jump back onto the couch, Grandma rushed out and snapped the radio off. We sat in silence the rest of the day, the only sounds the click of her crochet hook. My head throbbed.

After ten days, Mother came to get me. Grandma disappeared into the bathroom and didn't speak to either of us. After Mother shut the door behind us, I made a remark about Grandma. Mother grimaced. "Huh, she made you feel real good, too!" Before we left, she tore the warning off the wall. Rain had soaked the red sign causing the color to bleed, leaving streaks dribbling down the siding.

~ ~ ~

"Oh Roberta. No!" I was back in school less than two weeks before Miss Spencer again stopped beside my desk. She stared at my face and sent me once more to Miss Thompson's office. Chicken Pox. While Dr. McCandless hammered a new red warning over the stained spot on the wall, I walked past him, through the door for another ten days with Grandma Larson.

The nights turned bitterly cold and snow fell. Daddy's boots crunched as he passed our window at the end of the day. Each afternoon I etched designs of Rapunzel's castle with my finger in the frosty pane, hoping he would see it, but my design smeared into frost again before he walked by.

One afternoon as my finger drew through the frost, a face popped up in front of mine—a large, stuffed Santa Claus. With a grin Daddy peered around it. He bobbed it up and down like a puppet, mouthing words, letting Santa tell me that he belonged to me. Daddy used his daily coffee nickel to buy chances on a punch-board in the café and was ecstatic when he won the Santa. (A punch board was a large board with covered squares. Each square could be purchased, usually for a nickel. When punched, the square would reveal a blank, or the word "winner." That person received the offered prize.)

While I was quarantined, I couldn't have any of my toys or even a book with me, or they would have to be burned. I had to wait until I got well for Daddy to give me my Santa. Beaming, I nodded, understanding, and didn't even turn around when the bathroom door slammed.

Dogfish Island

❧

Things slowly became better between my sisters and me, perhaps for several reasons. After the kitchen knife incident, followed by the two bouts of illness that forced me to stay with Grandma Larson (one too many traumas for me), my spunky confidence collapsed into a fog of fears. I slipped in and out of cottony moments of disconnect and avoided people, even Daddy, unless we were alone in the greenhouse. That protective relationship had become fraught with too much danger when my mother or sisters saw me with him.

Maybe my Mother and my sisters observed me staying away from Daddy, minimizing my special role as his "real" daughter. Maybe my sisters began feeling sorry for me and softened as they observed my distress. But I think everything finally changed when Daddy beat me too.

I deliberately invited it, welcomed it, no longer wanting to be the spared one, hoping Mother and my sisters would accept me then. I did the forbidden: played with matches on the woodpile stacked against the washhouse, at a time when I knew Daddy would catch me. My bravado quickly dissolved, however, when I saw his rage. I fled into the house and hid under my bed, listening to him roar through the house demanding to know where I was. I crawled out, shaking, and began to run wildly around the house but he trapped me in their bedroom. Cowering, terrified, I looked up into his purple face and saw him raise his fists. But he became flustered, and his rage dissipated. After cuffing me painlessly several times, his arms dropped. When he noticed the urine running down my legs, he gruffly stammered for me to leave, but turned and fled himself.

Waiting outside the closed door in the adjoining room, neither Mother nor my sisters knew how my one and only beating unfolded, and I never confessed. I stumbled out of the room shaking, confused and sobbing—from emotion, not pain. I had wanted Daddy to hurt me like he hurt Marilyn and Ellin. Why hadn't he? I felt guilty with my secret. Even though I had provoked his anger and hadn't done anything to stop him, once again I had been spared. I didn't understand what had just happened, yet how relieved I felt. Then, to my surprise but as I had hoped—things did change. Although she remained cold and distant, Mother no longer accused me of being spared, and my sisters began to include me. I welcomed no longer needing to avoid them.

That June, when Marilyn turned 16 and Ellin was 13, even though I was only 8, they invited me to tag along with them to Dogfish. The island was called Dogfish because its shape at one end looked like a dog's head and the other like a fish's tail. At least that's what Marilyn told us.

Our property bordered Mud Creek, a gentle stream that ringed the five-mile circumference of this island before forking into the larger Cottonwood River that flowed through the town. Ancient black walnut and elm trees clustered along both sides of the creek, and a hay meadow anchored the center of the island, a meadow dotted with white clumps of Queen Ann's Lace and golden faces of sunflowers, tilting toward the sun. The creek was aptly named, the water dense and muddy brown, with thick foliage along its banks that provided a haven for poisonous copperheads and water moccasin snakes, but for us it was the safest place we had, and we thought it all wonderful.

Every day, as soon as we could get away, we raced across our family's alfalfa field and headed for the shelter of the woods. Entering the trees, we heard the purling water of the creek, the songs and conversations of red-winged blackbirds, blue jays, and orange-breasted robins, fluttering among the branches, sounds that merged with the crackling of weeds and twigs as we tramped through, every sound magnified in the silence. As we approached the stream, the dry, dusty smells of the field and grasses melded with the atmosphere of wet muddiness, along with the fetidness of rotting logs half-buried in the muck along the bank (another favorite place of the moccasins). Our hearts lightened as we slipped into the darkened coolness of our sanctuary.

Our island became our one neutral place, the place where we had the safety to romp free and play. I became acquainted with Marilyn's intelligence and strength, her gentle leadership qualities, and I respected Ellin's shy reticence to assert herself, and saw how she always looked to Marilyn for what to do. Any uneasiness I initially harbored going with them dissipated as I experienced their protection on occasions when I could have been hurt.

To cross Mud Creek we had to creep across the dam located behind the town's waterworks plant. Barefoot and clutching our shoes, we inched the narrow algae-covered cement wall over which the greenish water poured, spuming and frothing twelve feet below before rippling into the flow of the creek. I loved the sounds, the smells, the excitement. Before starting across, I'd often lie on my stomach along the dry section of wall and press my face close to the water, dangling my fingers in its murkiness. Small fins darted below the surface, and a water snake or two coiled away. I imagined myself sliding down into their mysterious, shadowy world.

Sting nettles grew lush in the fertile black ooze on the other side of the dam. As we clawed our way up the bank, if we brushed against the nettles' serrated leaves our bare legs and arms erupted with a burning rash. Marilyn showed us how to scoop handfuls of mud to spread on our itchy limbs, a trick she learned from a book on Indian lore. As our fingers dug into the muck, we unearthed tiny shells, and occasionally, arrowheads.

The first time we found an arrowhead we examined it with awe, running our fingers along the crude, jagged points someone had carved into the flint. We knew Indians occupied Kansas years ago. Marilyn studied them in school. They were called the Kanza Indians, she told us, which meant the "south wind people" for whom our state was named. We assumed it was the Kanza Indians who dropped their arrowheads on our island.

We rinsed our shells and arrowheads in the creek, stashing these treasures in tin cans. If we had a penny, we added it to our can before we buried it beneath a tree, marking the location on our treasure map. We had made our treasure map on a piece of paper, and had traced the path, starting at the dam, and numbered the trees so we could locate our burial spots. For each spot we colored a star. We called these places our sacred burial grounds, imagining they might have been for the Kanza people, always hoping to uncover bones of one of the Indians. Only rarely did we find any bones, and then tiny ones, probably of squirrels or rabbits. Marilyn kept our map rolled up in a cigar box under her bed. Our buried treasure represented our sacred bond, perhaps also a symbolic stake of ownership of this island that we now claimed as ours.

Sheltered among the forest trees, we splashed and swam in the creek, shimmied up trees, and ran freely through the wildflower-filled meadow, never glancing back across our family's alfalfa field that would lead us back home. But when the sun lowered and the shadows of the woods deepened, we trekked silently along the path back to our house, filling with our own dark shadows.

One Saturday afternoon, Marilyn and Ellin took me to the movies to see *Tarzan, King of the Apes*, played by Johnny Weissmuller, a gentle man with amazing strength and humorous wit. He kept his wife, Jane, and son, Boy, as well as his jungle with all its animals safe from any attacks. Tarzan's anger erupted only when necessary to protect. The family worked and played together. Protecting one another was their way of life, their expression of love.

For the rest of the summer our island became an African jungle. Marilyn assumed the role of Tarzan, Ellin became Jane, and I played Boy, always accompanied by our make-believe chimpanzee, Cheetah. Day after day we acted out our heroic adventures, protecting one another and our island from imaginary bad guys.

One day Marilyn announced we couldn't swing through the trees like Tarzan because we lacked forest vines. We needed the next best thing, a rope. Pondering how we could earn the money for one, Marilyn remembered hearing some boys talk about a dealer on the edge of town who bought scrap metal. That was exciting because we knew where we could find scrap.

Every day we carried buckets and walked along the railroad tracks, gathering bolts and other pieces of steel shaken from the trains. Whenever we heard the whistle and felt the rumble of an engine, we rushed to the side, our bodies vibrating as the gushing steam locomotive and clacketing cars thundered past. We waved our arms wildly to the engineer leaning out the window. Waving back, he pulled his lever, blasting the whistle twice. As the train whooshed past, we motioned and shouted to the agent standing on the porch of the caboose. He'd tip his hat, then spit tobacco juice over the railing.

One afternoon we watched the train disappear around the bend, the three of us transfixed, staring down the empty tracks. Marilyn's face hardened. "One day I'm going, too," she declared.

Each time we gathered enough scrap to fill one pail, we carried it to the dealer who weighed it on his scale, then counted out our money. Marilyn kept this in a shoebox under her bed. When we thought we had enough, we walked together downtown to the hardware store. Marilyn stepped forward, her hair slipping from behind her ears to cover her eyes as she lowered her head. "We want rope—to make a swing." The manager watched her hands tremble as she tipped the shoebox, emptying our coins onto the counter. "Do we have enough?" The three of us looked at him eagerly, waiting for his answer.

He carefully counted our money, sorting it into neat stacks, glancing at us as he worked. When he had counted each pile, he smiled. "You have just enough." He cut a long length of his strongest rope and handed it to Marilyn. We thanked him and rushed out the door.

Back in our woods, we walked back and forth along the creek to choose the perfect tree. Rolling the rope around her shoulder, Marilyn climbed up and tied one end to a branch, letting the rest dangle to the ground. She instructed Ellin and me to hang onto the rope and bounce up and down, to make sure it was secure.

Taking turns, she and Ellin soared across the water, Marilyn going first, yodeling her Tarzan call, before dropping onto the other side and tossing the rope back. Ellin cautiously followed, her smile broadening with each successful flight. When they told me I was too little to swing across, I protested loudly that I wasn't a baby, but only for a moment.

Every day we played out our stories of Tarzan, Jane, and Boy. But after that Saturday afternoon when we saw the second Tarzan movie, *Tarzan and the Amazons*, our imaginations leaped into a whole new dimension.

The movie introduced us to the Amazon women and their numinous city built entirely of gold, hidden deep within the jungle and inhabited solely by women. Skilled goldsmiths, they not only had constructed their golden city but also had filled it with magnificent golden treasures and had adorned themselves with golden jewelry. Tarzan, who had proven himself a trusted friend and protector, was the only outsider allowed into their kingdom.

Caught in unbearable suspense, we watched the story unfold, as a group of men, led by an archeologist, searched for this hidden city. A kind but naïve man, the archeologist had heard rumors of its existence, and idealistically hoped to reveal it as one of the last unknown cultures in the world. He remained oblivious to the evilness of the men he hired to help him, not realizing their intent was to plunder. He ignored the warnings that we kids, who packed the movie house, shouted to him.

The men worked their way through the jungle accompanied by natives who carried their supplies. When the archeologist succeeded in finding the connecting bridge and prepared to cross into the city of gold, the natives fled in terror. They knew no intruder ever left this place alive. Two of the natives rushed to alert Tarzan.

In the darkness of night, the intruders crossed the bridge into the city and located the treasure room. Swinging through the trees, Tarzan arrived just in time to alert the young girl on guard, who struck the golden gong. All the Amazons swarmed out, armed with bows and arrows. With Tarzan blocking the bridge at the other end, they trapped the men as they tried to escape with the treasure. The archeologist, realizing what he had done, fell from the bridge to his death. By the end of the movie, all of the intruders had been killed, and the treasure restored. The Amazons were safe.

Our new script was set. Transformed into strong and skilled Amazon women, we ruled over our golden island kingdom. The dam became the bridge that connected the outside world with our hidden one; our buried cans became the treasure stalked by greedy men. We chopped willowy limbs to string for bows and cut stiff branches for arrows. Splicing dandelion stems together, we created necklaces, bracelets and rings. We tucked the golden flower heads into our hair and every opening in our clothing. Over and over we created our versions of the story, the indomitable warrior women protecting our secret golden domain.

ᘉ ᘉ ᘉ

One afternoon late in summer, Marilyn and Ellin had gone somewhere without telling me. They seldom left home. Where had they gone? Why hadn't they taken me? I sat alone, pouting, feeling increasingly angry. I would get even and show them I didn't need them either. I would convince Richard, a new friend, to go to Dogfish Island with me. I had never gone without my sisters, and although I knew it was our special, secret place, it was something important that I knew about and Richard didn't. Besides, I wouldn't betray any secrets, just take him there. I pressed Richard, stressing how much fun it was, until he finally relented. We started off across the field.

Richard had moved into our neighborhood earlier that summer. He was nine, a year older than me, but appeared younger. Slight in build, pale-skinned and timid, Richard avoided the boys and chose me as his playmate. He became my best and only friend and we often played together.

At first, I liked going to his house. His mother's attentiveness charmed me, something new I hadn't experienced before. But then it became irritating. Accustomed to parents never aware or caring where I was or what I was doing, free to do as I pleased, I soon chafed with her attempts to control our every move. Yet I returned, fascinated with Richard's erector set. I wanted one desperately but knew I couldn't ask my parents to buy it. We had no money for an expensive toy, and, besides, people thought erector sets were just for boys.

While Richard slumped on the sofa, I spread his set out on the floor, filled with joy as I figured out how the parts fit, screwing nuts and bolts with the tiny screwdriver and wrench and attaching steel beams. "Come help me," I'd coax. Richard would roll his eyes and sigh, looking away. "Okay," I'd finally say. "Let's go to my place." He jumped off the sofa and helped me scoop the parts back into the box.

Hearing us leave, his mother would lean out the kitchen door. "Richard? Where are you going?" She never looked happy when he told her. "Well, you be careful now, you hear?"

Every day Richard wore immaculately pressed white shorts with blue suspenders stretched over crisply ironed short-sleeved shirts. His skinny pale legs looked ridiculous sticking out of the starched shorts. The neighborhood boys, wearing scruffy jeans and tee shirts, laughed at him. Richard would shrink back, staring at the ground, and sometimes run away. He refused to climb into my tree house, afraid he'd skin his knees going up, or fall out once he got there, and he wouldn't sit on the ground in my hideout under the spyrea bushes for fear he might dirty his white shorts.

I became impatient, yet in spite of everything, Richard was someone to play with. Except for the boys in our neighborhood, who let me join them after supper to play kick the can in the street, no one else in town wanted to play with me. I didn't know why. I had become too scared by then to go to anyone's house anyway, except Richard's, even if I had been invited. I only went to school and Sunday School. The only place Marilyn, Ellin and I felt safe together was on Dogfish Island. I felt safe with Richard, too. We were together every day and I knew he would never hurt me or make fun of me. I was his only friend.

The one thing Richard did like to do was sit in the backseat of my parents' car, parked in our driveway under the big shade trees, where he kept clean and stayed out of the sun. There was no room for us to play in my house and Mother didn't let me play with friends in the greenhouse. In the car, we read books from the library or made up stories, elaborate plots I no longer remember. But I do recall how his stiff shorts billowed, revealing that Richard never wore underwear. That summer, sitting in the car, I caught my first glimpse of a boy's privates. I stared. At first, I felt excited peeking, but soon it didn't seem so special. His shriveled tiny penis looked even more silly than his skinny white legs. I was glad I didn't have one of those things hanging between my legs.

When we arrived at the dam, we took off our shoes and socks and—gripping his hand and providing constant encouragement— I led Richard along the cement to where the water overflowed. We began inching our way across the slippery surface. Richard clutched his new school shoes in one sweaty hand and my hand in his other, his face pinched with fear. We were halfway across when he dropped one of his shoes in the water. We watched it slide down into the froth below.

Richard began to cry. Confidently, I assured him I would get it. Leading him back to sit on the bank, I found a long stick and crept down the dry part of the dam to perch at the edge. Leaning as far as I could, I reached out my stick over and over trying to catch the shoe, which was still tumbling, trapped in the froth, only to watch it disappear again into the turbulence. Finally, in spite of all my efforts, it bobbed free and drifted downstream. I watched it float away in disbelief.

Wearing one shoe and one sock, Richard limped along the gravel road as we walked silently to his house. He stood beside their back door, hanging his head. "Richard? Is that you?" his mother called from the kitchen. "Supper's almost ready. Come on in and get washed up."

He opened the door and slunk inside. I remained in the shadows, and heard his father burst into a rant. His father sold tires at the hardware store and screamed how many sets of tires he would have to sell to buy Richard another pair of shoes. I ran home, hot with shame.

The next day Richard came to my house to tell me he couldn't play with me anymore. We stared at each other in shared misery. I felt sick with regret and told him how sorry I was that I took him to Dogfish. Looking at the ground he nodded and left.

A month after school began, Richard returned to tell me they were moving. His father couldn't sell enough tires in our small town. He said one day he would come back and marry me. I tried to kiss him goodbye on his cheek, but he, flushing, stumbled backward, turned quickly, and ran home. I had never kissed anyone; no one had ever kissed me. I stood bereft, wishing he had let me. I needed to know he forgave me for urging him to go with me to Dogfish, for not having saved his shoe. But I think I simply wanted to say a special goodbye, knowing I would never see him again.

ᴥ ᴥ ᴥ

One day as we three Amazon women walked along the path, checking out our kingdom, Marilyn shouted out. The bow of an abandoned rowboat lay visible among the underbrush, the back half sunk in the creek mud. We slid down the bank to inspect it.

At first glance, our spirits sank too. It looked like an unsalvageable wreck. Faded gray paint hung loosely along the exposed wooden sides. Everything seemed to be rotting and falling apart. Marilyn knocked and prodded, felt underneath, then looked up hopefully. "It feels more solid than it looks," she announced. "Let's pull her out."

We started using sticks to dig out the debris, but tossed those aside to claw with our hands, heaving chunks of mud over the side. "An oar!" Ellin exclaimed. "And here's the tip of another one." We slipped and splashed in and out of the water, each of us caked with slimy muck, exposing more and more of the buried half of the boat. As it began to rise in the water, our spirits rose with it.

Ellin and I clambered up the bank and each took a side of the bow; Marilyn remained in the water to shove from the back. Together we pulled and pushed, paused to scrub away more mud, then continued to tug and shove. Finally wiggling the boat loose, we heaved it onto the upper bank and collapsed onto the grass. "Oh my gosh, we did it!" Ellin gasped.

Marilyn inched her way around the sides, smoothed her hands through the remaining slime, and traced along the boards inspecting every seam. "Well, we'll have to clean it up and test it in the water to see if it leaks, but I think she's a real honey."

"A real honey," I parroted, patting the boat.

We could hardly believe our good fortune. The boat obviously had been abandoned. We found it, we worked to save it, now it belonged to us. Exhausted, we surveyed our treasure, aware of a new and deepening, sweet closeness.

The sun hung low on the horizon, soon to disappear behind the trees. We slid our boat into tall weeds and piled up additional branches to hide it. Wading into the water to rinse off, fatigued to the point of giddiness, we looked at each other, then burst into hysterical laughing and splashing, until finally soaked, bedraggled and completely spent, we crawled out onto the bank and collapsed.

"Well," Marilyn gasped, "If anyone asks, we'll just say we went for a quick swim and forgot to take off our clothes." Looking at our appearance, once more we dissolved into giggles. Quieting, we reluctantly rose and tramped across our family's alfalfa field that led us home.

Shadows of dusk deepened into darkness before we arrived at the back door of our house. Whispering, we rinsed off with the garden hose, then crept inside to strip, towel off and pull on clean clothes before slipping into our places at the supper table. Daddy drooped in his chair; Mother, her body heavy with exhaustion, stood at the stove dishing up food. Neither seemed to even notice us. Peeking at one another, taking deep breaths of relief, we hungrily picked up our forks.

The next day we lugged a piece of packing rope, two pails and a scrub brush, and ran to our boat. Pulling it from its hiding place, we secured the rope to the bow and slid it down the bank. For several hours, we dipped buckets of water from the creek, scrubbed and bailed until our boat was clean inside and out. Tossing our supplies onto the bank, filthy and dripping, but ecstatic, we pushed the boat into the water and climbed aboard.

Marilyn sat on the middle seat to man the oars. Ellin kneeled in the bow, proclaiming herself our navigator, clearing the way by brushing aside low-hanging limbs, while I sat in the back, trailing my fingers in the water. Drifting downstream, carried along by the ripples, we three Amazons observed our kingdom from a new perspective. Gliding under uprooted trees, which from the path had appeared to be a mass of snarled roots, were now transformed into intricate domes of graceful arches. Even the clusters of sting nettles growing along the shores shone with a new beauty, the sun's backlighting glossing the edges of their serrated leaves into luminous shades of green.

I hung over the edge of our boat to swirl patterns across the water's surface behind us, watching them float away. Fishy smells from the stirred waters mingled with the humid, hazy air, the sun patching through overhead leaves to warm our skin. Everything blended into an afternoon of intoxicating pleasure. As often as possible we would escape into this magical world in which—united, unafraid and filled with power—we became free to relax and dream. Each night we carefully hid our boat in the underbrush, in our specially chosen spot.

It was with shock and disbelief when one day we discovered our boat had disappeared. Could we have forgotten where we left it? We walked single file along the path, poking into the densest foliage and checking the inlets along the creek. It was simply gone. We stared at each other. Suddenly, Marilyn held up her hand, signaling us to be quiet. Voices. Her finger to her lips, she motioned us to duck down into the weeds. Lying on our stomachs, as the voices drew nearer, we peered out, and watched three boys row past in our boat.

When they passed us, we crept low, following them. Around a curve, they pulled the boat out of the water and hauled it up the bank into bushes, far from where they had found it. As they scrambled up the bank to the path, we overheard snatches of their plans to return the next day.

After they disappeared, we stood up slowly, then slid down the bank. We listened for sounds, making sure they were gone before we tugged the boat into the water and headed upstream. Marilyn and Ellin laughed boisterously. We had won! We hid the boat farther away, in brush so thick we couldn't detect it ourselves as we paced back and forth, scrutinizing it from every angle.

The next afternoon we hid near where the boys had left the boat and waited. The three returned, laughing and swaggering down the path. They peered into the bushes, then fell silent. They poked into nearby brush, walked up and down the path searching, but finally gave up and left. "Shit!" one said as they disappeared down the path. We ran to where we had hidden the boat. Heaving it into the water, we clambered aboard and headed in the opposite direction.

Cobb's Barn

The tension between Marilyn and Daddy had become worse that summer. Mother bought a train ticket for Marilyn to spend two weeks with her aunt in Idaho. During Marilyn's absence, Ellin and I felt uneasy going to Dogfish without her, so we tried to think of a different place where we could escape, a safe and secret place just for us.

I remembered that Cobb, our retired old neighbor, had told me I could play in his field with my friends any time I wanted. Sharing this with Ellin, I announced that the field must include his stone barn at the end of his pasture, the building he used only to store his car and assorted old rusty tools. We ran to check it out, climbing the rickety ladder to peek into the hayloft. Perfect.

Stuffing sandwiches into our pockets, we took two brooms and a rope from our garage. Ellin suggested it would be fun to make a seat in the barn cupola. We rummaged through the woodpile for the right board—one that was the right length, not too splintery, and sturdy enough to hold both of us. Loaded down, we set off across the field.

The barn ladder wobbled as we struggled our supplies up and pulled ourselves up, through the trapdoor and into the loft. Breathless, we surveyed the shadowy space. The air smelled musty. Murmuring pigeons huddled on rafters, their droppings littering the floor. Cobwebs, heavily laden with dust, dangled from the rafters, and years of blown-in dirt formed tiny mounds across the floor. In the dimness, sunlight pierced through cracks around a small wooden hay-door at floor level, through which workers would have tossed bales of hay in years past. A narrow shaft of light from the cupola formed a rectangle in the middle of the floor. When we unlatched and pushed open the hay-door, sunlight flooded in. Pigeons whooshed above our heads as they rushed out through the open cupola. Feathers floated down, one landing on my hair. I touched its softness and showed it to Ellin. We traced the delicate black and gray-shaded markings, and carefully placed it on a low rafter. This was our first treasure in our new little world—a world that felt miles apart from our real one.

Hearing the start of the car below, Ellin and I poked our heads down through the trapdoor and yelled, "Hi, Cobb!" Without looking back, he waved his hand through his car window as his dented green Chevy lurched out of the barn, jerking and sputtering down the gravel driveway. Waving in return, we called, "thank you!" But he was far down the drive.

Together we swept the cobwebs and floor litter out through the hay-door, chattering our plans while we worked. We would ask Mr. Schmersey for orange crates from his grocery store to use for furniture, and we would paint a sign with big letters to tack onto the trapdoor: "Private Club." It would be our very special hideout.

The cleaning finished, we hauled up the ladder from below and positioned it so we could climb up to the cupola. Ellin coiled the rope and hung it around her neck. She went first, each of us grasping an end of our board and inched our way up the ladder, rung by rung. When Ellin reached the top, I pushed the board from behind as she heaved it across the cupola frame and wiggled it into place. Clutching one of the posts, I climbed onto our board seat. Ellin secured the rope she had carried up with her to one of the cupola's posts, climbed onto the seat beside me, and pulled up the rope that we would later use to slide down. She kicked the ladder away. "Yes!" we both yelled into the air, directed at a squirrel on a nearby branch.

Grubby but elated, we sat side-by-side swinging our feet into the open space below us. With grimy fingers, we pulled smashed sandwiches from our pockets, licking peanut butter oozing with grape jelly from the torn waxed paper. It all began to feel like our treasure house. Part of our plan for the next day was that we'd poke a tin can filled with treasures deep in a corner of the barn's eaves, under one of the floorboards, and tuck in our pigeon feather beside it.

Sweet, warm June breezes drifted around us. Unperturbed by our presence, a pair of wrens darted in and out above our heads, building a nest of twigs in the tip of the cupola. Perched high in our fortress, removed from everyone, Ellin and I believed ourselves secure in our own little nest.

When we noticed the sun lowering behind dark clouds hovering along the horizon, we headed home. In the growing gloom, a sudden breeze stirred the meadow grass. Shivering, we hurried across the field. Our family was going to a Shirley Temple film that evening. Shirley Temple was Ellin's favorite. People often said she looked like her, with her short, rather chubby build and natural curly hair bobbing around her face. She had a rich singing voice as well, one that people heard in church. Ellin would blush when someone called her "Little Miss Temple," and, though pleased, remained shy and tongue-tied.

As we trotted onto our property, we noticed our parents waiting by the sidewalk. Daddy stalked to the woodpile and grabbed a 2x4 board, then waited, his body poised in a tense crouch. We slowed. As we drew nearer, he sprang forward, snarling. "I don't want you over there!"

He began waving the board in the air toward Ellin, the two of them circling each other. She started running, trying to skirt around him. He raced after her, whipping the board across her back and legs, telling her to shut up when she screamed. Mother and I followed slowly. They disappeared into the house.

We stared at the door. Mother turned to me, her eyes glowing. "Next time it will be you," she said, her words harsh and brittle. She went into the house, slamming the door in my face. I stood outside, numb, listening to the board smacking against flesh, to Ellin's wails. Then silence. Dusk deepened into darkness.

Eventually, not knowing what to do, I tiptoed through the doorway and stopped at the edge of our bedroom. I peered through the darkness, heard Ellin's muffled sobs. I wanted to go to her, but my body froze. I couldn't step past my fear.

I slipped into my place at the table. Daddy slouched deep in his chair, staring at the table vacantly. Mother stood by the stove, watching her spatula stir back and forth through the scrambled eggs. No one spoke. Mother brought the skillet to the table, dumped eggs onto our plates, then clattered the cast iron onto the stove. She dropped a loaf of bread in the center of the table. We ate in silence. Without a word, we rose and drove to the movie theater.

Hours later I crept into our bedroom, dimly lit by an outdoor post lamp. Buried under her quilt, Ellin appeared as a shadowy cocoon. I touched her shoulder. She lowered the blanket and lifted her face. We stared at each other. She turned the covers back to reveal her legs, covered in welts, then rolled so I could see the bruises on her back. The stench of stale sweat and urine rose from her sheets. My stomach churned. She reached out her arms and we embraced, clutching each other. "Was the movie good?" she whispered.

I couldn't remember any of it. "It wasn't as good as the others. You didn't miss anything."

She remained in bed for several days, too injured to move, too bruised to be seen. We never returned to Cobb's barn.

Disappearance

When Marilyn returned from her visit, we three sisters ran back to Dogfish Island, but everything was different. Marilyn had changed. We didn't play our make-believe games. She rowed us along the creek while wistfully telling us about Idaho, how beautiful everything was, how kind her aunt had been to her. She told us about the government-sponsored program for teenagers where kids could train for technical jobs. If you passed a test, you could be admitted into the program even though you hadn't finished high school.

Hot summer days gradually cooled into autumn. School began. Our days filled, yet whenever we could, the three of us returned to our island. We slid our boat into the creek and bobbed lazily along with the current, watched the leaves turn color, felt the crisp in the air, each of us lost in our own thoughts.

Then one day I returned from school and found Marilyn and Ellin gone. Their things remained in our room, but those disappeared too some days later. My parents moved through their work like robots, their mouths set in a grimace. I knew something bad had happened, but my parents never talked about my sisters' absence, never even mentioned they were gone. Neither of them seemed to notice the two empty chairs at our supper table.

At first, I thought Marilyn took Ellin and ran away to Idaho. I remembered that afternoon at the railroad tracks as we watched the train disappear, when she vowed that she, too, would leave one day. Maybe she wanted both of them to enter that training program. But they would have taken some of their things. I tried to think of any other reason they would suddenly disappear. Then I knew, with a growing certainty. This time my sisters had done something that made Daddy too angry. This time he had beaten them to death. Whether he meant to or not, it was the only explanation. Their bodies must be buried somewhere in our field, probably in the back, among the deep weeds. I was too scared to search for freshly turned earth.

A bitter cold set in early that year. I slept alone in the bedroom I had shared with my sisters, their empty beds a constant reminder of their absence. Then one night I woke to a noise outside my room. Steady. Rhythmic. Relentless. Knock – knock – knock.

A few nights before, I had listened to *Inner Sanctum*, a radio program, in which the main character had been murdered by a trusted acquaintance. From his grave, the victim swore vengeance. He would haunt the murderer at night with his footsteps: step – step – step. Steady. Relentless. Knock—knock—knock. It was Marilyn, returning from her grave to haunt us.

The knocks returned every night; I dreaded going to bed. Turning stiff with fear, icy drops dripped down my neck dampening my pajamas. Curling into a ball, I retreated into my covers like a snail and peered out into the darkness, vigilantly tracking any shadow. Every morning, foggy with sleeplessness, I dragged off to school.

Spring eventually thawed the landscape. Mother again could hang the wash outside on the clothesline, which was connected from the washhouse to the corner of my bedroom. As I helped pin the clothes to the line, the knotted end, dangling from the hook on the wall, swayed rhythmically in the breeze. Thick with ice, with the winter winds the knot would have thumped against the house. It had been the frozen rope that kept me awake! Still convinced my sisters lay buried in our back yard, I felt relieved when I realized Marilyn hadn't returned from her grave to haunt us—at least not in this manner.

I never asked my parents about my sisters' disappearance. I knew better; no one in our family discussed these things. I longed to understand so much that remained beyond my grasp: these secrets our family never talked about—the long silences permeating our days, the dark nights haunting my mind, and I wondered whether or not other families lived like this—carrying in their hearts unspoken and unanswered questions wrapped in shame.

Anna and the Kolaches

◦⌒

One night during supper, Daddy told Mother the vacant house across the street had finally sold to an elderly couple from a nearby Mennonite community. They were retiring from their farm and moving to town. Daddy went to the cafe every morning for coffee and liked announcing anything new he heard. He swelled with importance and looked at Mother who, as usual, busied herself with the food and ignored him. He deflated, and we all lapsed back into silence. Inwardly, however, I perked up. I had been watching that little house ever since the former owners moved away more than two years ago. Over time, the house grew shabby with neglect and seemed sad, the For Sale sign almost lost among the weeds. Frequently, I had crept onto its porch to reassure it that someone would buy it soon. Now I returned to pat the porch wall, happily telling the little house that someone was on the way.

Watching for the new owners to arrive gave me something to think about, instead of my sisters. I sat under our black walnut tree and waited. Two days later, a white-haired couple and two younger men drove into the driveway of the little house. The woman disappeared into the house, while the men pulled ladders and pails out of the back of their truck.

Over the next two weeks, the three men transformed the entire property, painting the house a sunshine yellow, then adding apple-green shutters onto the sides of the windows. They cleared the weeds and scraggly bushes, mowed the lawn, and planted new shrubs and flowers. The woman came outside to wash the windows, scrub the front porch, then pour the dirty water around the new plantings. The day the younger men carried in the furniture, the older man painted his name and house address on a black mailbox mounted on a post beside their sidewalk: Fred Klein, 505 Walnut Street. The woman tied a bouquet of dried orange, gold, and red flowers to the front door. When everything was finished, the four of them stood looking at the house and each other, nodded and smiled. The younger men patted their father on his back, hugged their mother, climbed into their truck, and drove away. That night, lights shone from the windows.

I waited a few days before knocking on their door. The lady responded, holding the screen door open. She inclined her head and smiled down at me, speaking with a heavy accent. "Well, well, I have first visitor to welcome me. My name is Anna. What your name?" I told her, twisting my toe back and forth along her welcome mat.

Her thick white hair was wound into a ball at the back of her head, loose strands sticking to sweat along her neck. She had brilliant blue-grey eyes that seemed to look right inside me, as though she could see everything, and when she smiled, her weather-browned face wrinkled into a wreath of pleasant creases. "Well, I was wishing for company. You want come in? Today I bake. I make kolaches. You know them?"

I shook my head as I stepped into their living room. The dark brown sofa and two chairs, clustered around a braided rug, looked comfortably lumpy and worn. A round table, with a crocheted tablecloth, was covered with framed photographs. When I paused to look at them, Anna stood beside me and proudly told me about each one. She picked up the picture of two rigid people standing side-by-side, staring straight into the camera. "This my Fred and me on our wedding day. Oh, we were so young." She sighed, shaking her head with a smile. There were photos of both their parents, their two sons with their wives, and many pictures of their grandchildren. "Oh, they all so good to us. Our oldest son and his family move to our farm now."

I wondered what Daddy and Mother looked like on their wedding day. Mother had started a photo album, but there were no pictures of their wedding, not one of them individually or together. She put in a few photos of me during my first years, one of my sisters. There were none of my grandparents. I never heard about any of them, other than Grandma Larson, Mother's mother, who sent a card every Christmas with just her name and later lived in our backyard apartment. Mother kept the album beneath the pile of jumbled towels, sheets and blankets in their bedroom closet. I found it one day, disappointed there were so few pages filled. I stared at one picture of myself as a baby. I looked so unhappy. Mother had written underneath: "One year old. Sick with whooping cough." In the photo, my sad eyes stared at a cake with one candle burning. I softly touched her face.

Sunlight flooded Anna's kitchen. Its walls were freshly painted white, and yellow curtains swayed in the breezes of the open windows, one panel snagged on the leaves of a green philodendron setting on the sill. In the middle of the room stood a wooden table covered with flour, a rolling pin and an assortment of brown crockery bowls, measuring cups and wooden spoons. "You like help me?" Although shy, I felt her warm welcome and said yes.

I had never helped anyone cook before, not even Lizzie, where I just watched. Mother worked all day in our greenhouses and rushed in at the last moment to throw together our meals. She needed me out of the way. We ate hurriedly so she and Daddy could return to work.

Anna showed me where to wash my hands while she rummaged in a drawer for another apron. She looped it over my head, and when it dragged on the floor she giggled, folded the fabric high under my arm pits, then tied it in back. Her crinkled smiling face shone as she looked me over. "Now we ready."

Anna's stove had two ovens and two side compartments for warming, and all the doors were white ceramic speckled with dark blue. She opened one of these side-doors and pulled out a large crockery bowl filled with dough that puffed high above the rim. She pressed my hand against the side so I could feel its warmth. "This where my dough stays just right so it raise," she said.

She dumped the dough into the middle of the flour-covered table and punched it a few times, reducing the high mound into a flat piece. As Anna worked, thick purple veins bulged along the tops of her hands and forearms. Her fingers clutched, squeezed, and folded the dough, tossed it in a half circle, then clutched, squeezed, folded and tossed, over and over. Finally, she paused, breathing heavily, and pointed to the small bubbles appearing like tiny blisters under the dough's surface. "Now it ready," she said, wiping her face with her apron.

She began pinching off clumps, encouraging me to do the same, and showed me how to roll these round and round the palms of my hands, shaping each into a smooth ball before placing it on a large baking pan.

"Now this for you to do." She showed me how to press my thumb, just the right size, she said, deep into the center of each ball. I bent over my task, carefully centered my thumb above each puff, held it stiffly straight, and pressed ever so gently until I felt the pan underneath. When I had done the first one, I raised my head and looked at Anna. Her face creased into a huge smile, nodding her approval.

When I had done them all, she said: "Good! Now we fill the holes you make for us." She pulled two jars of jam from her cabinet, one with strawberries, the other thick with chunks of peaches. "From farm garden." Together we spooned the fruit into the indentations, all those empty spaces filling with sweet, sweet jam.

The aroma of baking rolls filled the room while Anna washed and I dried the dishes. She reached two blue plates from her cabinet and laid them on the table with two blue cloth napkins and filled two glasses with milk. "My son bring from our cows fresh this morning." I had never held a cloth napkin before, or any napkin, or sat at a table neatly set for each person. Mother would slide the stacked plates onto the table and throw the silverware into a pile, leaving each of us to sort out what we needed, while she plopped down the cooking pots filled with our food onto the middle of the table. I watched Anna carefully to know what to do next.

When the buns had finished baking, I held the oven door open while Anna slid out the pans. The jams oozed over the tops of the rolls, crusting into red and peach-gold globs of sweetness. "Here, sit, sit. Now we enjoy our hard work."

I perched on my stool. Anna slid two kolaches, one of each fruit, onto our plates before pulling up a chair to sit across from me at the wooden table. Rich layers of pale, yellow cream had risen to the tops of our glasses of milk. I picked mine up and dipped my tongue in to slowly push the cream around the rim before curling it into my mouth, then took my first bite of the roll, its warm yeastiness and sweet strawberries mingling with the cool cream. Anna watched my surprised delight and clapped her hands, her face crinkling into that big smile. She seemed to find pleasure in everything I did. I loved this little sunshine house.

"You and me—we bake more things together. You come again soon, my new little friend, yes?" Anna took both our aprons and hung them side-by-side on hooks behind the door. I skipped across the street, my heart singing.

🙠 🙠 🙠

Before I could return to Anna's, rainstorms pummeled the Midwest leaving floods in their wakes, inundating the valley in which Marion sat and reaching our house. I waited in a boat with the Red Cross volunteers and watched the water rise to my parents' waists as they stood in our driveway. Mother was arguing with the men, refusing to leave our property. They finally agreed Daddy and Mother could stay with the Griggs, who could make room for them in their two-story house across the street. The volunteers tugged my parents into the boat, rowed them to the Griggs porch, then continued with me to the end of our street, through the submerged downtown area, and across the bridge to the water's edge at the hill. One of the volunteers there drove me to stay with an elderly widow who lived on the hill—many people had offered to take evacuees into their homes.

Days later the waters receded, and although it would be many more days before any of us could occupy our houses that were flooded in the valley, a Red Cross volunteer drove me to see my parents. She said in such circumstances children and parents needed to be reunited. We slushed through streets coated with water and sheets of mud, devastation everywhere. As soon as I climbed out of the car I turned and skittered down our driveway to cross the street. It wasn't my parents I needed to see. I stopped.

Anna sat on their slime-covered sidewalk beside the mailbox, slumped against the post. Caked with mud, her hair straggling around her smeared face, she clutched two mud-soaked family photos. Her shoulders rocked back and forth. Brackish water oozed from the windows of their home and down the yellow walls. In one of the shrubs beside the porch wedged a bloated pig.

Their sons stepped out of their house. One held his father's arm. "Come on, Pop. We can't save anything." The other son gently lifted his mother and supported her into their car. They drove away and never returned.

A week later, I said goodbye to the kind widow on the hill and returned home. Everything was a mess. Our family lost almost everything, the greenhouses shattered, broken glass littering the washed-out benches. No growing thing survived. It took several weeks for the businesses along Main Street to clean up, order new inventory and open again; most of the storeowners themselves lived in houses on the hill. It took our family a full year to get back into business. Before I arrived, my parents had given our house a hose out, enough so we could exist in it, but after that they focused on the greenhouses. They cleared out the debris and Daddy glazed in new panes of glass before they could rebuild the benches and sow seeds. Agonizing months of repairs, then more months for the seeds to grow into saleable plants. That year we lived on oatmeal, and the few eggs from our chickens that had escaped the water to roost on the roof. On those days when my stomach rumbled, I remembered longingly those sweet-crusted kolaches Anna and I made that magical day. More painful, though, was how much I missed my new friend, but I would never see her again.

One afternoon a week later, feeling especially lonely as snow-flakes misted the frigid air, I gathered my courage and went to Dogfish for the first time since my sisters disappeared, uncomfort-able going alone but longing to know what the flood had changed or washed away. Was our boat still there? Our buried treasures? I jogged across our alfalfa field, leaving white puffs of breath trailing in the air. The leafless trees, stark silhouettes against the horizon, appeared like skeletons of Indian braves from the past, frozen in a frenetic dance.

I followed the path along the creek that once again flowed gently. Huge chunks of earth along the banks had collapsed, leaving roots of trees nakedly exposed. I shuddered, worried that if my sisters were buried in the back of our property, their graves might have washed out. Would I find their bloated bodies wedged in tangled brush downstream? An owl hooted softly, over and over, each call answered with a soft hoot from far away. When the owl stopped, silence echoed back among the trees.

In the steel-gray winter light, I forced myself to move on. I searched for our boat but gave up. It was probably miles downstream. Returning to the dam, I counted the trees beside the path, and located one of our burial spots. Poking through the smattering of snow with a stick, I jabbed the frosted soil, unearthing the tin can, and knocked the mud-clogged contents loose against a stump. Everything tumbled out, stinking with the odor of flood. Among the tiny white shells lay an arrowhead, and one of our pennies. The penny had corroded, the edge disintegrating into grit as I rubbed it in my fingers. I scooped everything back into the can and threw it into the creek, watching it bob along the surface until it gradually sank out of sight.

New Girl

❧

Weeks after school began a new girl joined our third-grade class. Carol sat at a desk nearest the windows, across the room from me. She remained quiet, speaking only when asked a direct question. Carol was the only colored kid, not only in our school, but in our entire town. The other kids stayed away from her. They weren't mean toward her. They just didn't want anything to do with her. Over time, I learned this didn't bother her. She seemed comfortable with her differentness. We started meeting during recess on the playground, where she told me she had no brothers or sisters and that her dad worked with a gang on the railroad. She became my closest friend.

One afternoon Miss Gray, our teacher, announced we were going to begin learning how to multiply numbers. She handed out a sheet with the first two of the multiplication tables and told us to take it home and be familiar with them by the next day. I looked at this strange bunch of figures and felt the familiar fear. Miss Gray continued explaining, demonstrating on the blackboard, but in spite of watching her lips and straining to follow her words, I simply couldn't understand her. Becoming increasingly anxious, suddenly I shut down and was gone. At home that night, I stared at that page of numbers but didn't know what I was supposed to do with it.

The next morning in class, I couldn't follow what Miss Gray was saying to us, but when everyone got up and went to the blackboards, I followed, taking my place beside Dale, a boy I knew only by name. We picked up our pieces of chalk. Dale scribbled on the back of his hand then rubbed it off on his jeans. Miss Gray dictated something for us to write on the board. I watched Dale and wrote what he wrote. He stuck his tongue out at me. "Very good," Miss Gray said, glancing around the room, and gave us two more numbers. I listened to the squeaking of chalk around me and fumbled with my eraser. Dry, gritty white dust clung to my fingers. I tried to wipe it off on my dress, but it didn't absorb the particles like Dale's jeans did. Dale glanced to see if Miss Gray was watching, then grinning, smacked two erasers together in front of my face. I jerked away from the cloud of dust. Dale smothered a laugh. I hated him, hated all of this.

He wrote more numbers. I copied them. Glaring at me, he cupped his hand so I couldn't see his work. I looked back at Miss Gray. She was watching me. My face turned hot as I dumbly faced my section of the blackboard. I wished I could stand beside Carol. She would let me copy her numbers. I glanced down the line of students and saw her at the farthest board. She was studying the blackboard, frowning. After giving us several more problems, Miss Gray started around the room, looking at our work. With each student, she responded "Good!" "Yes!" or "Almost. Good try." Miss Gray paused when she saw my blank space, then moved on. I hung my head. "Very good, Dale," she said. He smirked at me. I lay my chalk in the tray at the bottom of the blackboard and turned my back on him.

During recess, Carol and I shared our blackboard experience. Mumbling, I flushed and confessed I hadn't understood anything.

"Why do you feel so bad?" she asked. "You just haven't gotten it yet, but you will." She had done only two of her problems right, but she accepted that she was behind in knowing what to do sometimes, having gone to so many different schools. "Every morning my mother tells me to do the best I can, and I'll be fine. She tells me not to worry, because I'm smart and I'll catch up." I listened to this in wonder.

One morning Carol invited me to go home with her after school. From our lunch break on I watched the clock, growing more excited as the hands slowly moved toward three-thirty. When the bell finally rang, she and I walked to the far edge of town, then crossed the railroad tracks into a small area where the streets were dirt, there were no sidewalks, and most of the paint on the houses was either peeling or gone. The yards were littered with trash and tree limbs still from the flood, plus a few broken cars. Her mother opened the door when she saw us coming, her smile just like Carol's, spreading across her entire face, clear into her eyes. She and her daughter hugged together, rocking back and forth playfully, then pulled me close into their circle. Her mother lay her hand on my shoulder and looked into my face. "Carol's daddy and I are so glad she met a good friend here."

They lived in what was probably the shabbiest house in the poorest section of our town. They drew their water from an outdoor well and used the outhouse in the back, their few pieces of furniture threadbare, the rooms almost empty. I noticed but didn't care. I felt their home's warmth, smelled its goodness, and thought it beautiful. Carol's mother, Mrs. Wallace, wrapped a towel around her hands and removed a sweet potato pie from the oven. I had never heard of sweet potato pie before, which Carol couldn't believe. "Mama fixes this for us all the time," Carol said.

"It's more a colored people's food," Mrs. Wallace added. "Your mama probably makes you pumpkin pie." She was a large-built, buxom woman with dark ebony skin that had a luminous glow. Like her kitchen, everything about her was clean and neat, her rose-colored housedress starched and ironed, her straight black hair held back from her face with a pink band. She smelled of baby powder, soft and sweet, and she radiated kindness and strength.

She sat with us at their kitchen table and cut three pieces of the warm pie, listening to Carol chatter about how confusing multiplication problems were, how she needed to work on them later that night, and how I felt bad for being slow to understand them. I felt my face redden and slowly slipped lower into my chair. Mrs. Wallace continued putting pie on our plates and pouring glasses of milk, not jumping in with strong words of encouragement. Instead she talked gently to us, words I no longer remember, but as her soft words warmly wrapped around us, I began to sit up straighter, and something new fluttered inside me: I began to believe it would be all right. Like Carol, I too might be smart enough to learn how to multiply numbers. Suddenly, overcome with an urge to climb onto this mother's lap and nestle into her full sweet-smelling bosom, a yearning that became so deep it turned into a pain that caused my eyes to grow misty, I lowered my head and concentrated on my pie.

I never invited anyone to come home with me. Our house was too small to play there, but most of all it was neither comfortable nor welcoming. My parents always were in the greenhouses, where Mother didn't want us hanging around bothering the customers. I went home with Carol almost every day, where we played and studied together, slowly mastered our multiplication tables and learned how to multiply. Mrs. Wallace always had a freshly baked sweet potato pie waiting for us. She'd sit with us to share it, listen to our talk, and laugh with us. When we showed her our papers, she'd study them carefully, then nod. "I knew you both could do it."

One morning, Carol didn't come to school. Miss Gray announced to the class that she and her family had moved. It wasn't unusual for railroad gangs to be told at the close of the day they'd be moving on down the tracks, probably during the night. I had never met her father, as he always arrived home after dark. He must have told his family they were leaving after I had gone home yesterday.

Carol's books and writing tablet remained in her desk. I stared in disbelief at her empty seat and felt hollowed out and numb. Then my hurt and anger rose. She left without our seeing each other one more time, without saying goodbye. I would never again go to their house, would never see her mother again. No one even told me they might be leaving soon. My angry disbelief left me hot and limp.

Then I thought of them. She would be missing me too, feeling just as bad as I felt. Carol's family had lived on the opposite side of town. They had no warning they were moving on last night, had no telephone, no way of letting me know. They must have had to grab a few things, leave their warm-smelling kitchen, their beds and most all else behind as they hurried to the railroad tracks to climb into those boxcars. Now they were rattling down the tracks far away. Were they huddled on the rough floor, cold and hungry? How could men order people around like that? I knew Carol was thinking about me, maybe at this very moment, missing me and our fun times together, missing her desk, missing her schoolbooks. I imagined her mother holding Carol tight against her sweet bosom.

I sat at my desk, very alone. I couldn't believe I'd never see Carol and her mother again. Everyone important in my life seemed to just disappear, without any warning.

~ ~ ~

Miss Gray, our teacher, was a tall prim middle-aged, large-boned unmarried woman, who never used make-up, kept her hair severely pulled back into a bun—none of the strands would dare straggle free—and every day wore a plain navy-blue suit with a high-necked white blouse and black-laced low-heeled shoes. I remained quiet and compliant in class, which she probably considered exemplary and why she gave me all A's on my report card. Most of the time I sat in our classroom in a haze, not even hearing what was going on. Still, even though I was never comfortable in school, I felt safe with her, until that day when—for the first time—I became a problem.

Every day at lunch Miss Gray gave each of us a pint bottle of milk, donated to the lower grades by the government through the Public Health Department. One day I had a severe cold and sinus infection, and as I bent over to drink from my straw, a huge glob of snot slid from my nose straight into my milk. I stared, nauseated, at the greenish-orange blob bobbling on the white liquid and pushed my milk to the far edge of my desk. Miss Gray walked up and down the rows collecting the empty bottles. Surprised to find mine still full—not noticing its contents—she told me to hurry, but I shrunk down into my seat, too embarrassed to show her what had happened. The other students left for recess, free to leave once they finished their milk.

As the moments passed, she leaned against her desk glaring at me, and began tapping her fingers on its wooden edge. I lowered my eyes. Why was I afraid to tell her? My head throbbed, so heavy. I just wanted to sleep. At the end of the recess she strode out of the room and returned in a few moments leading my classmates. She walked to my desk, glanced at my full bottle of milk, then marched to the front of the room.

She rang her bell. "Boys and girls," she began. She told us how privileged we were to be given milk every day while many children in the world didn't have any milk at all. "Roberta apparently doesn't understand this," she said, looking at me, her thick black eyebrows furrowed. Everyone twisted to look at me. "She'll drink her milk before she leaves this afternoon and will stay at her desk the entire recess period each day for the rest of the week. Perhaps that will help her remember to be thankful."

When the students left at the end of the day, Miss Gray worked at her desk, not looking at me. I stared at the bottle of milk, at the disgusting floating mass, then lay my head down and closed my eyes, my nose dripping steadily onto the sleeve of my sweater. The wall clock ticked thunderously, in rhythm with my pounding headache.

At 5:00, Miss Gray stalked over to me, grabbed the un-drunk milk and told me to leave. "I'm disappointed in you, Roberta," she snapped coldly.

She must have seen I wasn't feeling well. Confused and scared, I didn't understand what was happening, but realized I couldn't trust her. I wished Carol was still here, that I could tell her and her mother what had happened. I felt an empty ache when I thought of them. I drank my milk every day after that incident, but I remained on guard and counted the weeks until the end of school. Next year I would have a new teacher.

Summer Adventures

〜

That June I would attend camp for the first time. Back in second grade, all the girls had been invited to join the Brownies. Excited, I had taken the permission slip home for Mother to sign. She wrote the check for my uniform, then paused, her face sad. Marilyn and Ellin had so wanted to be Brownies, she said, but she and Daddy hadn't had enough money to buy their uniforms. "You've gotten all the breaks," she accused, and handed me the signed slip and the check. Even though they didn't have the money for my sisters to be Brownies, I wished Mother felt happy they could do it for me. I felt sorry for my sisters, and guilty listening to her accusation. When I got my Brownie dress, even though I felt so proud, I hid it in the back of the closet I shared with my sisters so they wouldn't feel bad.

Two years after our Brownie group was formed, when our class entered fourth grade (the autumn my sisters disappeared), we girls graduated into full-fledged Girl Scouts. Each of us received a handbook that outlined the program. It included the Girl Scout Pledge: to strive to live the ideals of honesty, fairness, and respect for one another, working together to make our world a better and safer place. My heart pumped faster every time I read the words. Here was what I had been searching for, a better way to live, a family community I could be part of.

As the summer approached, we prepared to go to Camp Mary Dell for the first time, the Girl Scout camp located outside Abilene, Kansas. Mrs. Hagan, our leader, told us we would join together with Scouts from all over the state, for one week becoming one large family of sisters. There would be activities such as arts and crafts, nature study and horse-back-riding. My excitement grew. I studied my handbook and practiced the pledge every morning in front of the mirror.

To earn money for my green plastic flashlight with the Girl Scout emblem, I pulled weeds and watered neighbor's gardens. We needed a flashlight to light our way at night, since we stayed in cabins scattered among the trees. Two days before we were to leave, I printed my name on each piece of clothing with a permanent pen and packed the required articles. On a balmy morning in June, along with three other Scouts, I sat in Mrs. Hagan's car as she drove us to Camp Mary Dell.

Every morning that week, we met at the flagpole to raise the American flag and recite the Pledge of Allegiance. Then for breakfast we trooped into the communal hall, an open, screened room with ceiling fans. Before we sat down on the long benches beside the wooden tables, like a prayer we recited the Girl Scout pledge. Each morning I had a lump in my throat as my voice joined the others in promising to unite as sisters and work together to achieve our Scout ideals.

In crafts that week, I learned how to weave colorful potholders, and I completed three as gifts for Mother. Spatter painting was my favorite craft activity. Placing a leaf or other object on a sheet of paper, I held a piece of window screening above it and brushed paint through with a toothbrush. When I lifted the item from the paper, I delighted in my colorfully outlined white designs.

We followed camp counselors down wooded trails to identify birds and observed habitats of raccoons, beaver and deer. The counselors taught us how to distinguish poisonous snakes from harmless ones, although we never saw any of either kind. Three times that week, I took my turn at kitchen duty, peeling mounds of potatoes and learning how to nick out the eyes—something no one bothered to do at my home.

What I loved most of all, though, was horseback riding. We hiked the dusty road to a nearby stable where they paired each girl with the right horse for her. Every day I rode a gentle brown mare named Caramel, who patiently tolerated my learning how to hold the reins with the right tension as I urged her into a canter. At the end of each ride, I wrapped my arms around her neck to bury my face in her mane. "My sweet sweet Caramel apple," I'd whisper, and rubbed her muzzle.

On the surface, our days were ideal, the camp picture-perfect. After supper each evening, we lowered the flag, and then we sat around the campfire roasting marshmallows and listened to our counselors tell inspiring stories of women who performed heroic deeds. Finally, we joined together singing camp songs before we headed back to our cabins. My favorite was *White Coral Bells*, always the last song. The leader divided us into three groups to sing it as a round.

Walking back to our cabins, we lighted our way with our green Girl Scout flashlights while continuing the song. The girls ahead on the paths started the first round, and those at the end finished it, their final notes fading into the silence of the night as each group reached their cabin. Every night I fell into bed exhausted, deliriously happy. I was in love with camp.

Our camp didn't have a swimming pool, so one hot muggy afternoon our counselors took our group to a nearby creek to cool off. While we romped and splashed in the water, the counselors lay in the shade of the trees above us, deep in conversation. As they chatted, they looked down occasionally to check on us. The humid air clouded hazily, redolent with the river aromas of algae, fish, and muck.

Then a girl discovered the frogs. She squealed with delight. Quickly the others joined her, racing to capture the frantically leaping creatures. Trapping the frogs into a small circle, the girls began ripping the frogs' legs off so they couldn't hop away. Bodies quivered and flopped about on the ground. Even dismembered, they continued desperate efforts to escape. Torn-off legs jerked and trembled.

"Mexican jumping beans!" one girl shouted. The other girls shrieked and laughed, then ran along the riverbed searching for more.

"Over here! There's a whole bunch." They returned with fistfuls of young frogs, grabbing and shoving each other aside.

"Let me have that one! I haven't done one yet!"

"Yes, you did. I saw you."

Our leaders glanced down but continued to stretch out in the grass.

"Stop it," I told a girl as she tore off a leg, my voice trembling. "Don't do that."

"Oh, Miss Goody-Goody. Or are you scared? Here!"

She threw a limbless body at me. What was left of the frog landed beside my bare foot and flipped over, its live eye looking up at me. I stared at its quivering muscles trying futilely to move, and I began to cry. Then sob. Suddenly the counselors were sliding down the bank toward us. The girls stopped giggling.

"Get rid of the frogs," one hissed. Scrambling, the girls scooped as many parts as they could and threw them into the weeds. Some jerking legs and one body remained. A girl tried to kick them aside, but the counselors just stepped over them.

"I have no idea what's wrong with her," a girl answered the chief counselor. "We were only playing around in the water and for no reason she just started crying." She glowered at me.

The counselors hovered and asked me what was wrong. One tried to put her arm around my shoulders. I pulled away. I knew they had seen those frog body parts, and probably had been watching the entire torture process. Why hadn't they stopped the girls, and why did they now pretend they hadn't known? Their concern rang so phony. They simply hadn't cared. I turned away from everyone, continuing to cry.

"We'd better head back," the counselor said to the other.

At the camp, our counselors sought help from the director. "She's probably homesick," the director said. "After supper, we'll have a special campfire."

I knew it wasn't homesickness, but I couldn't stop crying. A deep pain gripped my chest so hard I thought I couldn't breathe. I tried to stop. I wanted to stop. I couldn't understand what was happening inside me, and I stood apart from the other girls, struggling helplessly to choke back my blubbering, aware of the girls staring and whispering.

We sat cross-legged in a circle around the campfire. With exaggerated gaiety, the director led us in our favorite songs. I flooded with embarrassment, understanding this was all because of me. The kitchen crew brought trays loaded with Graham crackers, marshmallows and Hershey bars, and the counselors showed us how to roast S'mores. They moved from girl to girl, handing out seconds. I couldn't eat my first, and sat dangling my roasting stick in the flames, watching the marshmallow melt and slowly burn away.

"She's such a baby—just wants attention," sneered an older girl. "They should send her home."

I wished I could go home. I wanted to leave all of them, to go to bed, but my counselor wouldn't let me walk back to my cabin alone. Finally, after the campfire died to glowing embers, everyone went by flashlight along the wooded trails to our cabins. Although all seven of my cabin mates and I had been a comfortable group before, they huddled together now at the far side of our room, whispering and sending me disgusted looks. One girl looked over and said loudly, "What a brat." "Spoil sport," added another.

I heard the director's footsteps on our porch outside my window, heard murmuring voices as she talked with our counselor. "Let's see how she is in the morning."

I muffled my grief into my pillow, lying still a long time before falling asleep. I knew our counselors had seen what the girls were doing to the frogs. In the presence of this violence and suffering, those who could have stopped it remained silent. Nothing was different here. My excitement about joining this sisterhood—committed to the ideals of kindness and honesty—shattered. I lay in my bed feeling completely alone.

At breakfast the next morning, I stared down at the table and didn't join the other voices when they recited the pledge. The director paused beside my chair, bent down, squeezed my shoulder, and said she was glad I was feeling better. I remained wooden, not responding to her. She patted my head and moved on. All day I remained on the fringe of my group, barely participating. It wasn't hard to do, since no one wanted to be around me, either. For the remaining two days of our week, I was ostracized, but I didn't care.

On our final afternoon when I kissed Caramel and said good-bye, burying my face in her mane, tears slipped down my face. I knew she understood. She was the only reason I didn't want the week to end. I would miss her, my only friend.

The next morning, we packed our bags and piled into cars. I chose a backseat corner and stared out the window all the way home.

∽ ∽ ∽

Following camp and wanting to be alone, most afternoons I went to the library to lose myself in books. Mrs. Ray, the librarian, never objected to my lying on the cool granite floor in front of the oscillating fan in the children's section. I loved the faint mustiness that greeted me as I pushed open the door, the quietness, the soft whir of the fan. Years before, unable yet to read, I studied the picture books stacked along the bottom shelves. Sometimes I brought my teddy bear, leaned him against a chair, and, if we were alone, I would tell him the stories as I turned the pages. His black button eyes absorbed every word.

Now, day after day, I lay on the floor in front of the fan and read. I turned first to the Bobbsey Twins series. Although far too young for me, and I had read most of them before, I now read several again, envious of the fun this family had together. Most of my time, though, was spent with Nancy Drew. I fell in love with her stories and dreamed what it would be like to be her: an only child whose mother had died, beloved by her successful lawyer father, pampered by their housekeeper, plus she had her own sporty roadster to zip around in while she successfully solved the mysteries in her life. When I finished all of Nancy Drew, I dipped into the Hardy Boys, clever and fun guys, who had constant adventures and never tortured animals. I imagined they were my brothers, who would go to Dogfish Island with me, like Tarzan ensuring everything remained safe. As the summer drew to a close, I thrilled to my first of Zane Gray's novels, stories of cowboy heroes in the wild west who protected good people. I had fallen in love with reading, and when I sank into a story, it carried me away from everything. I began to look forward to school, to my new teacher, and I hoped she would assign us new books to read. But my summer experiences hadn't ended yet.

～ ～ ～

Scowling at their lawnmower, abandoned after a single swath of cut grass, Mrs. Griggs, hands on her hips, angrily muttered that—once again—her oldest son, Otis, went off with friends without finishing his job. I had come to visit. "I can do it," I quickly volunteered.

"You would do this overgrown mess? You're kidding. How old are you?"

"Nine, but I'll be ten in October. I'll be in fifth grade this fall," I said. I added that I mowed our lawn every week with the same kind of push mower.

She shrugged, laughed, and threw up her hands as she went into the house. "Go ahead if you want to."

I forced the mower through the long grass, struggling across their front yard. This was harder than I thought it would be. After only two rows, I hit a stick that shattered and flew into the air. The thick half of the stick remained wedged in the blade, jamming it. I jiggled the mower back and forth unsuccessfully, then reached down and pressed the blade to force it free. Releasing quickly, it jerked forward and trapped my thumb. Quickly, I pushed the blade the other way. Blood gushed.

I clutched my gashed hand and stumbled home. Mother found me leaning over the bathroom sink, holding my bleeding thumb under running water. When she lifted it to look at the cut, we saw bone through the gaping flesh. My knees buckled. Everything turned black. Mother supported me while reaching into the cabinet for the box of cotton. She squeezed my thumb hard, blood soaking wad after wad. Keeping pressure on the cut, Mother continued to sop up the blood until it was a tiny trickle, then wrapped my thumb tightly with cotton that she fastened with adhesive tape.

"How in the world did you do this?" When I explained, she said, "Well, did you learn never to put your hand in a lawnmower blade?" The gentleness in her chiding voice surprised me, and looking up into her eyes, I saw concern. As I watched her wipe up the blood, everything again turned black and I collapsed. She grabbed me, eased me onto the toilet seat and pressed my head forward between my legs. When I felt steady enough, she guided me to the sofa and helped me lie down, encouraging me to close my eyes and rest. She showed me how to prop up my thumb to reduce the bleeding. I listened to the rattle of pans and opening of the refrigerator door as she started supper. My thumb throbbed; the pain made me nauseated.

Daddy came in from the greenhouse, scooted a chair across the floor, and sat beside me. He placed a roughened hand softly on my forehead. At his touch, tears dripped onto my neck. Leaning close, he whispered for me to come with him. My superhero Daddy had returned.

He drove us downtown and parked the car in front of Al's Cafe. "You and I are going to eat here tonight." My schoolmates raved about Al's thick, juicy hamburgers. I had longed to taste one, and sometimes peered hungrily through the windows of the cafe on my way home from school. As we walked in, the mingling aromas of burnt grease, coffee and stale cigarette smoke hit me like a slap. Smoke rose in hazy clouds above booths raucous with laughter. The fluorescent lights seared into my headache. Daddy beamed when he reminded me that I once said how much fun it would be to swivel on the black-leather stools by the counter. He guided us to them now. I steadied my throbbing thumb and half-heartedly tried to twist back and forth, but it made me dizzy.

Al walked over to take our order, wiping his hands on the splattered towel tied around his waist. Daddy ordered not a hamburger but a cheeseburger for me. "And Al, bring extra dill pickles." Noting my bloody bandage, Al nodded. He asked Daddy what he'd like. Daddy said he wasn't hungry. "Just a cup of coffee."

Al set the cheeseburger in front of me. Leaning forward to look into my face, he said he added three extra pickle slices. Rare juices oozed from the meat, staining the bun red. I turned away, feeling bile rise in my throat. "I'm sorry," I choked.

Daddy patted my arm. "Let's wrap this to go, Al," he said. "Be sure to include those pickles." Picking up the bill, Daddy counted out the exact coins. Puffing his chest, he slid a nickel beside his coffee mug.

At home, not bothering to undress, I curled up in my bed and tried to elevate my pulsating thumb, tears sliding down to soak my blouse. I never tasted that cheeseburger. I hoped Mother cut it in half so she and Daddy could share it for their supper.

Gradually my thumb healed. I could move it slowly after the first weeks of school, and eventually, hold my pencil again with my finger and thumb instead of with two fingers. I sat at my desk and traced a finger over the clean scar that extended almost the entire circumference of my thumb. I marveled at my mother. She couldn't afford a doctor for stitches, so she attached the severely cut, loose end of my thumb to the bottom of my thumb, taping it securely so it would heal in perfect alignment. In spite of so many things I couldn't understand about her—all our painful, confusing times—as I saw how my thumb worked smoothly, I wondered.

The Broken Rose

ᴄ❧

During that summer, on a typical Kansas July day, by mid-morning the heat shimmered in waves above our red-bricked streets. Hoping to avoid the worst of the heat, Daddy and I loaded the deliveries into our navy-blue Chevy paneled truck. We stopped first at the local hospital (my favorite delivery spot) five rooms located above the Gas Company and the shoe repair shop on Main Street.

Daddy and I carried three bouquets of garden flowers up the dimly lit wooden stairway. Sweat ran down his tanned face as he nudged the screen door open with his elbow, securing the door with his foot, while he balanced a vase of flowers in each hand. Hurrying to hold the door, Vera, the head nurse, reached for one of the vases.

"Lord, can you believe this weather!" she said. The ceiling fan labored to stir the air, its one crooked blade bumping each time it hit the dangling chain.

Whenever we went there, while Daddy took care of business and visited with Vera, I would wander down the hallway to stand on tiptoe in front of the nursery. Pressing my face against the window, I hoped to find a baby lying in one of the three bassinets. If there was one, sometimes Vera rolled it closer to the window so I could see the swaddled bundle of new life. A picture of Jesus hung on the wall, a kind-looking young man with long golden hair curling along his shoulders, his pale blue eyes gazing down at the new babies whom he embraced with outstretched arms.

This morning, turning down the hall toward the nursery, I stopped. A gurney was shoved into the corner behind the entrance door. My eyes met those of a woman, lying on the gurney, cradling a newborn baby. Her dark hair was frazzled and uncombed, her sweaty face tense. Eyes flashing, she pulled her loose hospital gown closer, and with effort, turned away from me to face the wall, clutching her baby protectively against her bosom. When Vera saw me looking at her, her smile disappeared.

"Why don't you go on down the hall and look in the nursery, honey? That baby girl's still there."

Born five days earlier, the infant in the nursery slept in her pink-lined bassinet. I stared at her for long moments before tiptoeing back down the hall. I glanced through the doors into the sterile white rooms, the raised metal beds waiting, sheets tucked squarely at the corners.

On our way home, I asked Daddy, "Why was that woman stuck behind the door?"

"All the beds must have been filled. There probably wasn't anywhere else to put her."

I remembered the bus accident a year ago, when all the rooms were full and additional beds were brought in to jam the narrow hallway. "But that's not true," I said. "Four of the rooms were empty. And there was only one baby in the nursery." Daddy stared straight ahead. We drove the rest of the way in silence.

That night at the supper table, still troubled, I told Mother about the woman I had seen behind the door with her baby. As she passed the bowl of boiled potatoes, Mother glanced at Daddy. He shrugged. "I think she belongs to one of those niggers that's working over on the railroad. The gang's been staying for the last week in those boxcars pulled onto the side track." He gulped half his glass of milk and belched. "She's lucky they even let her in."

I couldn't remember hearing that word before, strange and harsh sounding. I didn't know what it meant, but understood Daddy considered the woman an unwanted intruder. I recalled how scared she was, her eyes wild as she tried to shield her baby.

I felt confused. We had three colored people in our town: Al Holder, the barber; his sister, Lizzie, who took care of our neighbor, Cobb; and old Mr. King, who rattled up and down the alleys with his rickety horse-drawn wagon collecting trash. What was it about that woman behind the door? It couldn't be because she was colored, could it? The Holders were well respected, and everyone liked old Mr. King. But each of them was older, and unmarried, and they lived here. It must have something to do with this woman belonging to a man who worked on the railroad, just passing through our town. Or was it that she had a new baby? Why would Daddy think she didn't have the right to be in one of the empty rooms, and why wasn't her baby in the nursery? I thought of the picture of Jesus hanging above the two empty bassinets, the Jesus who welcomed all new babies. That same picture hung in our Sunday school classroom.

As I thought about all this and stared at Daddy's hardened face, something began crumbling inside me. It would take many years for me to grasp this moment and understand, but deep inside, even then I knew. All this time, in spite of his violent rages and embarrassing social behavior, I had clung to the gentleness I experienced with him. I continued to believe that, like those radio superheroes we listened to while working side-by-side in the greenhouse, he, too, stood for goodness and justice. As a vulnerable child, I needed him to be that father I could depend upon. Now, jolted, I realized he wasn't that man, and I would never find the answer to our family's suffering in his silence. I would have to figure the secrets out myself.

The following morning, pacing the driveway, I waited for Daddy to load the deliveries into the truck. At the hospital, I found the gurney gone from behind the entrance door. No one mentioned the woman or her baby.

Back home, I ran to the black walnut tree in our front yard and hauled myself up the rope onto my perch. Looking over the rooftops, I saw the railroad tracks two blocks away. Five boxcars sat on the side rail, their black roofs lustrous under the glare of the midday sun. I watched for a long time before sliding back down the rope. Running into the flower shop, I asked Mother if I could have one of the roses she received the day before.

In the heat of a Kansas July, long-stemmed red roses were rare and precious. They had to travel by freight train for three days from California or Oregon, and, to withstand the heat of the boxcar, they were wrapped in wet newspaper then packed in ice. Our local doctor had ordered a dozen for his anniversary. Daddy and I had delivered them to his wife that morning. I knew Mother always ordered two more than she needed, just in case. When I asked if I could have one, she gave me the rose that had arrived broken.

I hurried down the gravel road to the railroad tracks, sheltering the rose against my body to shield it from the sun. As I trotted along the uneven ruts, small chits of gravel worked between the straps of my sandals, and my feet stirred dust clinging to the sweat on my arms and legs. At the tracks, the acrid odor of burning tar rose from huge globs smeared along the wooden railroad ties, messy bits of tar sticking to my sandals. I hopped awkwardly from one tie to the next. In the stillness, I heard the slapping of my shoes against the ties, the drone of locusts screeching from clumps of weeds growing alongside the tracks. The searing heat beat against my skin.

I approached the first boxcar. Fumbling, I held the rose in my teeth while I stood on tiptoe, grasped the metal rod beside the door, and hoisted myself up the ladder. It was empty, shadowy and huge. The hot metal rod burned my hand. I dropped back to the ground and moved to the next car.

I found them in the fifth car. The woman lay naked in the far corner on a crumpled, stained blanket. Her baby nursed fretfully. The door on the other side of the car stood open too, yet there was no breeze and the air hung heavy and still. When she saw me, the woman clutched her baby tighter and draped the blanket over her thighs, her eyes smoldering across the empty boxcar. I heaved myself up, sliding into the doorway. The splintery floorboards scraped my bare legs. We stared at each other.

"You have a pretty baby," I said. She glanced warily at the door behind me. I wondered if she remembered me. The heat was stifling, the humidity saturated with a gagging odor. Insects swarmed the air around her blanket. "I have something for you." I placed my gift on the planked floor. The rose drooped, its petals bruised and discolored.

The woman stared at the rose. She lowered her face and nuzzled her baby. When she raised her head, her eyes brimmed with tears that slowly spilled over, creating tiny tracks through the dust on her cheeks. The space across the boxcar narrowed. I smiled. She smiled back.

I wanted to stay, yet my legs scorched. "I'd better go." The woman straightened, hesitated, then lay back with a nod. I have often wondered what she almost said.

The next morning the tracks stood empty, the rails gleaming in the early sun. I sat in my tree perch, a painful sensation gripping my chest: the hollowness of being left behind. Aware that I had violated an unspoken code, I never shared this incident with anyone.

Rebellion

❧

That autumn I couldn't believe it. Because of administrative changes, Miss Gray had advanced with us and continued to be our teacher in fifth grade. I kept my distance, remaining the quiet, obedient student. My report cards continued to be filled with all A's.

One morning at breakfast, the emptiness of my sisters' chairs really bothered me, the tense silence around our table made me want to scream. Why didn't Mother or Daddy ever talk about them? What had happened? Were they dead? If not, where were they? The familiar pain churned in my stomach. I shoved my oatmeal aside. "The one time I didn't eat all my oatmeal," Mother said menacingly, "my dad got a big spoon and stuffed it down my throat. Maybe that's what I should do to you?" My anger ready to explode, I slid off my chair and didn't look back as I stomped out the door. Walking to school, I kicked every black walnut on the sidewalk out of my way. My stomach hurt.

We pledged allegiance to the flag and sat down at our desks. Miss Gray announced we would begin something new that morning—cursive writing. She gave each of us a workbook, in which each letter of the alphabet was demonstrated, followed by two lined blank pages for our practice. She explained we would learn one new letter at a time, copying it over and over to fill the pages.

Heads bent over workbooks, the only sound in the room that of pencils moving across the pages. I picked up my pencil and began, filled the first line with A's, then stopped. My head ached and felt heavy. I didn't feel like doing this. I hated doing this. I stared at Miss Gray as she sat at her desk, absorbed in her work. Her prudish ways disgusted me. I hated her too, with her long nose and thin, judgmental smile. I hated my parents. I hated Marilyn and Ellin for leaving me. I shoved my writing book aside.

My desk was in the back row, nearest the door. I wanted to run out but knew I couldn't do that. I saw the door to our school library, a small alcove along the back of our classroom. I laid my pencil in the groove at the top of my desk, checked again that Miss Gray wasn't looking, and slipped into the library. I walked back and forth in front of the long, single shelf before choosing *Black Beauty,* then crept back to my seat. Miss Gray hadn't moved. Shielding the novel, I opened to the first page and began reading. Dale glanced over at me and grimaced. I glared at him, sticking out my tongue and making a face. I hated him, too. During every writing practice, I repeated this routine, smug in my refusal to do those stupid exercises, feeling superior, certain I had hoodwinked stupid Miss Gray.

Weeks later, Miss Gray strolled the room during our final writing practice, glancing at each student's progress. I dropped the library book onto my lap and leaned over my workbook, bending my arm to hide the blank page. She paused beside me and said softly: "Tomorrow I will collect everyone's completed workbook." I sat stunned. Collect them? She was going to look at them?

That afternoon I smuggled my workbook under my shirt and ran home. Icy drops slid down my neck as I turned to my first and unfinished "A" page and began copying the letter. Mother came from the greenhouse to prepare supper, turned on the light, and told me to move off the table. I had just finished the letter G. Shaking my stiff fingers, I knelt beside the piano bench and began H. Bolting my food, I knelt again beside the bench and began L. Mother and Daddy went to bed, Mother reminding me to turn off the light when I finished. I paused to stand, stretch my knees and shake the cramp from my hand, then moved over to the table and began "W."

Writing my final Z, I flexed my right hand, trying to work out the cramps, and rubbed my thumb along my scar that now throbbed. I checked to make sure I had completed every letter. Looking at my pages of hasty scrawl, regret settled over me. I wanted to write pretty, but all my letters were sloppy and shaped funny. I hadn't learned how to do them. If only I had done these exercises the right way. I hated Miss Gray even more. She had known what I was doing all along. It was her fault. She hadn't even cared when I went off on my own. Yet, I began to feel bad, the old guilt pushing in. In my anger, I had acted without thinking. I had always followed the rules at school, remaining fearful and compliant. But then I hadn't.

My stomach started hurting. My sisters and I had always been left alone to fend for ourselves. There were no rules, and I felt comfortable doing whatever I wanted, going where I wanted. But I had never gotten into trouble in school before. As I turned the pages in my messy workbook, I felt a growing fear. Anger had always been dangerous in our house; I learned long ago never to even feel it. But that one morning—what happened to me? I trembled. My world seemed overwhelming and dangerous. Had my sisters gotten too angry and rebelled too? Is that what happened? Why had they disappeared? And if it happened to them, could it happen to me? I felt right on the edge of something terrible happening to me.

I stared down at my desk when Miss Gray walked the aisle to pick up our workbooks. She didn't comment when she picked up mine and never talked with me about it afterwards. I received an A on my report card for reading, but my first and only D—for penmanship. This time she had given me the grade I deserved.

Perhaps Miss Gray was teaching me a lesson, perhaps not, but with the frightening absence of my sisters, plus my painful experiences earlier that summer, everything lumped together to leave an indelible mark on me: an awareness there was cruelty and danger not only in my home, but outside, too. Before this summer I thought I only had to escape my house to feel safe. Now I felt shaken and unsure of myself, and completely on my own.

My vigilance deepened, and I never wavered from the rigid restrictions I began imposing on myself. I received admiration as the proverbial "good" girl, conscientious and responsible, but my reality was that I had become a prisoner of my fears.

Hill and Valley

⌒

Marion was divided into two communities: hill and valley. The ridge of limestone cliffs defined this division, along with the Cottonwood River that flowed under the Main Street bridge a short distance below the cliffs. Even though there were scatterings of exceptions, this natural separation also formed the dividing line of our residents into two social classes.

Main Street ran east to west, from the east city limits on the hill, straight down through the commercial center of our town in the valley, to the west city limits. In the valley were the official county offices, located in the historical limestone Court House, the town's shops, banks, churches and the valley elementary school, lawyers and medical offices, and the city's municipal building that housed our library, an auditorium for performances, and its basement for large gatherings. Though a few professionals lived in well-kept beautiful homes, mostly the residential area of the valley housed blue-collar workers. They lived in houses that were older, with smaller sparse green space called yards (instead of lawns), and many of these houses showed the effects of the floods that periodically swept through the valley. The two railroads, the Santa Fe and the Rock Island Lines, provided the valley's borders on the west.

To socialize, some valley families belonged to the Oddfellows and met Saturday nights at their Hall, which consisted of rooms above the town's creamery, rooms reached by climbing steep, squeaking wooden steps. The women (the Rebekah's) sat on one side of the large room, sharing dessert and talking, while the men smoked their cigars and played checkers and dominoes on the other side of the room. Two or three times a year they had special events: square dancing, or performances by country music singers with their guitars. Two times my parents took me with them for an event. As the only child there, I spent the evenings withdrawn and embarrassed. I hated the cigar smoke, felt uncomfortable with these people I didn't know, and even hated the name. It made me feel we were "odd" just being there. I noticed none of the hill families were present, but my parents didn't socialize with any of them either. The hill women belonged to groups like bridge or literary clubs, or groups dedicated to community service. The men belonged to the Kiwanis Club and gathered at the country club for golf. At the Odd Fellow's Hall, Mother and Daddy, with forced smiles, awkwardly tried to join in, but usually left early, and afterwards they never did anything with anyone there. After a year or so, they quit going.

One Sunday afternoon, I found them lying in their darkened bedroom, which surprised me. They never rested; they were always working. When I asked if they were all right, after silent moments, mother sadly said they didn't have any friends. I tiptoed away, my chest gripped in vulnerability.

At the end of each business day, most of the people who worked in the town shops and offices got in their cars and drove to their homes on the hill, Marion's prime residential area. After crossing the Cottonwood River Bridge, Main Street branched off into Elm Street, but either street led up the hill. Going straight up Main

Street you passed our hill's elementary school, as well as the town's only junior and senior high schools. Continuing, right before the sign that said, "Leaving Marion," was the Marion Country Club with its canary-yellow club house, acres of golf course, and their spring-fed swimming pool. Here, hill fathers and sons played golf, people from the hill swam and gathered for parties in the clubhouse, at times dancing to the live ballroom music of the Stardusters, a band from Wichita. Few if any valley families belonged to the Country Club, although, when I was a senior in high school, my parents, like the parents of several of my valley friends, paid the $15.00 summer fee that allowed me to swim there.

Elm Street was the alternative access to the hill. The Presbyterian church, built in 1871 from native limestone, and the newer Christian church across from it, stood at the crest. Those marked the entrance to Marion's most prestigious residential area. Most of the houses were large and well-kept, tall trees providing cool shade. Their more spacious green spaces, called lawns, were neatly mowed. Our family belonged to the Presbyterian church because Daddy's father was a Presbyterian minister. Daddy seldom attended church, but each Sunday Mother drove the rest of us past the Baptist, Methodist, and Evangelical Christian churches in the valley to the Presbyterian church on the hill. We were the only kids from the valley who attended there.

In spite of feeling on the fringe, my experiences at that little church gave me roots that continue to nourish me. From my pre-school days in the basement Sunday school—joining the semi-circle of children on our little red chairs listening to our teacher Miss Jewell's stories—to the later years when we joined the adults upstairs in the sanctuary (each of us rushing to grab a place on the coveted smaller pew in the back), I grew to treasure words from the songs we sang, words that return to inspire me like beloved poems. From our childish voices in the basement, belting out *Jesus Loves Me* at the top of our lungs, to us as adolescents joining the congregation and listening to Jake Hein's deep bass voice booming across the sanctuary, setting the beat—"Come... come... come...come"—before the rest of the congregation joined in singing "to the little brown church in the wildwood," (words we knew referred to our little brown church on the hill)—these songs became embedded in the fiber of my being.

But it was Christmas that became my most precious memory. We began singing our favorite carols the Sunday after Thanksgiving, and the young people started practicing their parts for the Christmas pageant. Every child had some role in this candlelight celebration, that was filled with homemade costumes for the drama and the choir's special music.

After the candlelight celebration, everyone gathered in the basement hall for fellowship and refreshments. Several long tables held urns of coffee and hot chocolate, plus platters of colorful, buttery-rich traditional cutout cookies. The women baked for days in preparation, decorating each cookie with intricate details: silver bits creating sparkling stars, candy canes frosted with red and white stripes, and tiny decorated ornaments on the green frosted Christmas trees. The Santa cookies were the jewels though—not only their frosted red and white clothing and fluffy beards, but also each Santa's pack stuffed with individually decorated toys. Every platter was different, and over the years we learned to identify which woman had decorated which group of cookies, and (though no one confessed to such a thing) an element of competition hung in the air every year as to whose cookies would outdo the others.

The climax of the evening was Santa ho-ho-ho-ing and jingling down the back stairs, bursting into the room with his pack bulging with brown sacks of hard candies and nuts for each child.

We always knew it was our superintendent of Sunday school underneath that white beard, the father of one of my classmates, but we still shouted with excitement when he appeared. Later at home, my sisters and I sat on our bedroom floor and spread out the contents of our sacks to examine each piece, taking turns with the hammer to crack nuts, elated if we were lucky enough to get more than one of the big black Brazil nuts that we called "monkey toes." In the very bottom of each sack was the treasure—an orange—the only fresh fruit we had all year. More than all the sweets, for me that orange was the highlight of Christmas.

This celebration at the church *was* Christmas for my sisters and me. At home, we never shared any Christmas excitement. I have not one happy Christmas memory we experienced as a family. Not even this joyous holiday could penetrate the silent tension of our home. The excuse was that it was a busy season for our floral business, so our feeble attempts at festivities were quickly thrown together Christmas Eve after the shop closed. There was no time for cooking, so there were never aromas of special things simmering or baking. Mother decorated a very small tree or a plant from the greenhouse with a few ornaments and draped icicles, but because it crowded the room too much and we had to place it on top of our radio or in the middle of our table, we took it down Christmas night. My present on Christmas morning might be a book of paper dolls, but usually I received a pair of snow-pants or boots to replace those I had outgrown from the year before.

During those early years, my sisters and I remained outsiders at our church, even though the people were cordial to us while we were there. We sat side-by-side with the hill kids in Sunday school, sang together in choir, and performed the Christmas pageant, but once we drove back down the hill we never played with anyone who lived on the hill, nor were my parents included in any of their social events.

Although everyone in town remained friendly with one another, the lines of separation when it came to socializing and belonging to the various clubs and churches were clear and simply accepted as the norm. Kids from the hill and the valley only began to really get acquainted when we entered the one junior high school. When we started senior high, located across the parking lot from the junior high, the farm kids, after graduating from their rural schools, joined us. Yet we were still hill and valley. Valley kids dated other valley or farm kids, but hill kids mostly dated each other. Perhaps I felt the alienation more because—for reasons I never understood—I knew my family didn't belong with any group.

و و و

When I entered junior high school, merging with the hill community for the first time, I was completely vulnerable.

Every Friday, the whole school met for a general assembly, during which students could sign up to perform. Week after week, all through sixth grade and into seventh, I watched fellow students stand in front of this audience to sing, play an instrument, or recite a poem. Finally, I gathered my courage. I wanted to belong. I would try. I signed up to sing.

A new girl in our class played the piano and agreed to accompany me, a first for her at our school as well. Her father was the new minister of the Methodist church, so she lived in the valley too, in the parsonage a block from the church, though her father's status resulted in her being invited to join hill kids. Although we practiced at her house several times, during study hall the day before we were scheduled, we slipped from our classroom into the adjoining auditorium to practice where we would perform, not knowing the room was not soundproof. After doing our piece three times we grinned at each other. We were ready.

Brimming with confidence we returned to our classroom. The teacher stopped us as we entered the room, telling the new girl to sit down while making me stand in front of the class. Smirking, she announced: "Well, none of us need attend assembly tomorrow; we have heard this song enough and are sick of it." She turned her back on me, leaving me to slink back to my desk.

The next day I stood before the school sweating profusely, my face scarlet. I fumbled my way through my piece, mumbling the words while staring at the floor, then fled to my seat before the piano finished the last chord. Eyes smarting, I listened to the thin smattering of applause and wanted to disappear. I never performed again, in or out of the classroom, unless I was forced, and then it remained torturous.

Later that year, the music teacher held tryouts for all the parts in the junior high school musical, except for the lead role. She said she would choose that person herself. I didn't try out for any part, hoping to fade into the chorus. When the list of her choices was posted, everyone crowded around the bulletin board. Astonished, I saw my name beside the lead role. Two eighth grade boys, hill boys who were the most popular boys in school, stood in front of me scanning the list. One sneered. "Oh God, I don't want to be her brother." The other added, "Well, I sure as hell don't want to be her sweetheart!"

My voice was sweet and clear, but our rehearsals were a disaster. I felt the disdain of those two boys and froze whenever we shared a scene, unable to sing above a timid warble. Our music teacher became increasingly frustrated, yelling at me to stand up straight, to sing louder, to loosen up. Once, she flung down her musical score and stood with her head bowed. Why didn't she replace me? Children don't have the option of excusing themselves from impossible situations. She and I both suffered through.

Nothing improved the night of our performance. The climax of my embarrassment occurred when the boy playing my "boyfriend" made the noticeable point of refusing to hold my hand during the important final moment, and I heard the other kids snickering around us, having anticipated this.

At last the nightmare was over. No one talked to me afterwards, and I stung with the humiliation of knowing I had failed. All the scorn and rejection I experienced that year showed me our community simply wouldn't accept me. Regardless of how much I wanted it and had tried through the years, I was my family. I didn't know what was wrong, but like them, I didn't have whatever it took to be accepted. I, too, remained a lonely outsider. My confidence and spirit plummeted to zero.

Secrets

The summer before that disastrous seventh grade, Mother took me with her for the first time to visit her dad in Illinois. She made this trip every three or four years, in August when our greenhouses went dormant in the heat. When we drove into his driveway, Grandpa Scheffler came out to meet us. Everything about him scared me. A short, burly man, his every movement appeared abrupt and authoritative, conveying that he expected to be obeyed. His thick, unruly hair looked extra white beside his ruddy face, a face so red he appeared freshly sunburned. But it was his intense blue eyes with a gaze that pierced right through me, that made me uncomfortable. He greeted Mother curtly, then gave orders for one of his men to take our bags over to the family house. He turned and stood, looking me over. After scrutinizing me for what seemed forever, he gave a grunt, (I didn't know if it meant approval or disapproval) turned and strode across the parking lot to his office. I determined to avoid him.

Though not close, he and Mother had formed an amiable relationship. In spite of banishing her twice for going against his will to marry men he didn't like, he had taken her back both times. He still didn't like my father and wanted nothing to do with him—Daddy could never visit—but Grandpa had softened toward Mother. He invited her to return every few years to stay with him and his wife Rose in their comfortable house on the grounds of their floral compound.

During these trips, Mother visited with her half-sisters and their families and those hired men she had worked with who were still there and remained her friends. I heard one of her half-sisters remind Mother that Mabel, (my grandma Larson, Mother's mother) lived in a retirement home in the nearby suburb. Mother ignored this as though she hadn't heard. While we were there, she never went to visit her. Years before, while Mabel was living in our backyard apartment, one day she abruptly packed her suitcase and left on the bus, for reasons that remained unknown to me. Until this trip, I had not heard her name mentioned since.

During our visit, I watched Mother unfold like a tight flower bud in summer's warmth. The freer and faster pace of this Chicago lifestyle suited her. She became relaxed and responsive to the casual, liberal manner of her many friends there. I was introduced to a culture far different from the only one I knew, a small town in the conservative, Midwest Bible Belt. Mother had returned to her roots, her real home.

I liked Grandpa's wife Rose with her warm smile and ready, easy laugh. She introduced me to my cousin Chuck, a boy my own age, whose dad worked for Grandpa. Chuck came with him every morning while I was there, to keep me company. Rose slipped each of us a $5 bill—a fortune—telling us to have a good time. I observed how everyone respected and liked her, and that in spite of Grandpa's gruff appearance, Rose really was the one who ruled things, including him. She treated my mother and me with a welcoming hospitality. It was developing into a fun visit for both of us.

Chuck and I ran around together every day. He was a few inches taller than me and just as skinny. His thick black oily hair continually tumbled into his face, smearing his large-framed glasses, so he often stopped to pull up his tee shirt to wipe them and brush his hair back. We liked each other from the moment we met. I discovered I could run as fast as he could, even faster at times, and gloated watching him strain when we raced across the grounds. We confided that we both felt we had been friends for a long time, and I told him I pretended he was the brother I wished I had, though I got mad at him when he made fun of the way I talked. Each time we met one of his buddies, with a teasing grin Chuck would ask me to pronounce "town." I always did, then flushed when they guffawed, never understanding what was so funny. The way they said "town" in their Chicago clipped way sounded silly to me.

Grandpa was proud of his "five acres under glass." During these years, before an income tax was put in place, he had grown wealthy as the primary supplier of flowers to the Chicago wholesale markets. His hired men, the ones who were single, stayed in the large boarding house on the grounds in comfortable sleeping rooms, where they received excellent meals and good pay. He depended on them and made certain they remained happy.

While we were there, Grandpa hosted his monthly dance for all his employees, a large, noisy affair with free jukebox music, tables loaded with refreshments, and local girls who looked forward to this monthly event, too. I saw beer served for the first time. Kansas was a dry state and no restaurant served liquor, although we had a local liquor store on the outskirts of town where people quietly bought bottles to take home in brown paper bags. Even airplanes stopped serving alcohol while in the airspace over Kansas. I remained naive and innocent, never experiencing any kind of alcoholic drink, and believed beer was the beverage of sinners, found solely in the smoky pool hall on Main Street where girls never went, and boys that nice girls refused to date hung out. Once on the way home from school my girlfriend and I peeked through the pool hall door, and then ran away giggling and breathless, knowing we had stepped onto the threshold of Hell.

Surprised and delighted at the dance, I watched Mother laugh and dance with her friends. It was a new experience seeing her having fun, being popular and social, and, in turn, I began to feel a new freedom within myself. Then—I saw her drink from a bottle of beer. Seeing my shock, her eyes flashed. Loudly, with words cold and venomous, she spat out like a curse: "You're such a Newsom."

Everything quieted. People turned to stare at me. I stumbled backwards as though physically struck. What just happened? What did her accusation mean? I had begun to feel comfortable with her on this trip and hoped things were changing between us. People here were friendly and welcoming. Now it happened all over again, but different this time. She had embarrassed me before in front of people, but she had never attacked me quite like this. Now I realized her former recriminations—of being such a disappointment and Daddy's favored real daughter responsible for everyone's suffering—went even deeper: I was someone foreign and disgusting to her—a "Newsom." But still, what did that mean? She turned her back on me and strode away. I fled the silent, murmuring room, burning with shame and embarrassment, and ran to find Chuck.

Chuck joshed me playfully, making me feel better, until the two of us were once again racing around the darkened grounds. Hiding from him, I ducked through the parking lot—then stopped. Mother was sitting in a car with a man, his arm draped around her shoulders. She snuggled against his shoulder, lifting her face as they kissed. I stared at them from the shadows. Mother noticed me. She stopped smiling, lowered her head, and whispered to the man.

He beckoned me to their car window. Waves of musky after-shave scent met me. I noted his handsome face, his oiled brown hair shaped into waves, his smartly tailored suit with colorful shirt and tie. Digging in his pocket for money, he asked me to get them Cokes from the machine in the shop. His seductive, gleaming blue eyes penetrated mine as he slowly rubbed the coins back and forth, back and forth in my palm, then squeezed my fingers together with pulsing movements, over and over. I tingled with what felt like a surge of electricity, leaving me roused and strangely excited. He noticed, and chuckled.

I raced to get the Cokes and sped back to the car, eager to please this strange, attractive man. When they saw me, they laughed, shaking their heads. It had been a ruse to get rid of me. I flooded with embarrassment, feeling foolish. Not looking at their faces, I handed the Cokes through the window, threw the change into Mother's lap, and dashed away.

I told Chuck what had happened, except for how the man had stroked my palm. "Boy, are you a dope," he said. "Don't you know who that is? That's Henry, your mother's first husband. He just got out of prison. Boy, the Boss better not find them. That's why they're hiding out there in the parking lot. Rudy would shoot him."

A few days later, Mother sadly hugged her friends good-bye. On the train we remained silent, Mother retreating, cold and distant. I must have imagined that fleeting closeness I felt during the first days of our visit. Her contemptible accusation flung at me during the dance woke me to our true relationship. She hated me. Neither she nor I ever mentioned that trip. Back home again, it seemed never to have happened.

Daddy beamed as we stepped off the train and reached out to hug Mother. She turned her head away. I had never seen Mother kiss Daddy. On rare occasions. when she dressed up and he approached her, telling her how pretty she looked and tried to peck her cheek, she pulled away, protesting he would smear her makeup. At other times, she shrugged him off, saying she was busy. He seldom tried anymore.

Now his playful grin disappeared. I felt sorry for him, not wanting him to know about Mother being with Henry, how she had cuddled and kissed him, how happy she had looked. I wondered if he already knew.

I remembered the photo I once discovered in Mother's bottom drawer while putting away the folded laundry: Mother embracing an unknown young man in front of an early model Ford, the one called "the Tin Lizzie." He was tall, slim, darkly handsome and nattily dressed. Mother looked happy and stylish. Her short-bobbed hair framed her smiling face and she wore makeup and a string of beads with earrings. Her low-cut dress revealed her cleavage—I hadn't realized she had one. The caption underneath the photo said: "At least Lizzie is behind us." I stared at the picture, never having seen Mother like that.

Now I had seen her just like that, and I knew who the man was.

ഗ ഗ ഗ

The following November, one Saturday morning, Mother asked if I wanted to go with her to Wichita. I assumed it was to buy flowers from the wholesale market there, although Daddy usually made those trips. Was she going this time, and asking me to go along, to make amends? My hopes rose. But we drove the fifty miles in silence.

Instead of going to the market, we stopped in front of a large, brown brick building in the suburbs. A sign read: "Mt. Carmel Catholic School for Girls." Puzzled, I wondered what we were doing there. Mother opened the trunk and lifted out a plain frosted cake she had baked. At the reception desk, startled, I heard her ask for Ellin. A nun led us down a dim hallway and rapped on a door before opening it. "You have visitors," she spoke into the space, turned and walked away.

Sitting on her bed, Ellin looked up, surprised. She appeared so small and forlorn. Her room was bare, furnished only with a narrow bed with an iron bedstead, a scuffed chest of drawers and a tiny desk. A crucifix hung on one of the white walls; on the opposite wall hung a picture of the Virgin Mary, her head bowed sorrowfully. Mother breezed in with a fake cheerfulness calling out "Happy Birthday," then instructed me to go ask for a knife to cut the cake, and for some forks and plates. The receptionist phoned the kitchen and, once they were delivered, I carried everything back to Ellin's room. It was silent when I walked in. Ellin stood beside her bed. Mother was studying the view out the single narrow window.

During our visit, I never saw Mother look directly at Ellin, give her a hug, or ask how she was doing. There was no birthday present, and we never sang happy birthday. It was a brief stay, uncomfortable and awkward. When Mother and I prepared to leave, Ellin looked at me beseechingly. Overcome with confusion, I longed to hear what she wanted to say, ask what she was doing here, if this is where she had gone when she left home? How did she get here? Why couldn't she come with us now? She was alive, but where was Marilyn? Mother hurried me out. I glanced back at Ellin staring at us, sad and alone.

When I got into the car, I turned weak with a rising anger, filling with disbelief. All this time my parents had never once mentioned my sisters, why they disappeared and where they were. I thought they were dead. Why did Mother bring me here? She could have left me home and I would never have known about Ellin. Why did she bring me with her? She never talked to me or even looked at me the entire time. Once again, everything was secret. I thought of our silence with Ellin, how there had been nothing happy in this birthday for her. No one talked about anything. Did Mother take me with her so they couldn't talk, telling Ellin while I was out of the room not to talk with me there? My indignation boiled.

Mother and I drove home in cold silence, a silence that continued around our supper table that evening. As always, it was as though none of it had happened. Had Daddy even known where we went? Had he known all along where Ellin was?

⌀ ⌀ ⌀

How long after that visit to see Ellin was it that Mother asked me to go on a road trip with her again? Perhaps one year? She said she felt like getting away and wanted to go see the mountains in Colorado. We would have to go now in early autumn before the weather turned bad. Was this her way to reach out to me, to share something together that we might both enjoy? Again, I began the trip with hope, but soon realized nothing had changed. Preoccupied, Mother drove across the wheat fields of Western Kansas in silence. As the mountains emerged on the horizon, she brightened and said we were going to the top of Pike's Peak, a goal she had had for a long time.

When we began our climb, Mother maneuvered the narrow hairpin curves with an increasing speed and strange giddiness that frightened me. I stared out my window at the road's edge, appearing no more than a foot from my side of our car before the sheer drop into space. I clutched the sides of my seat and closed my eyes. At the top, without pausing, she turned around and headed back down, ignoring the spectacular view or the small crowd who had gotten out of their cars to absorb it. When we leveled off at the bottom of the mountain, she exhaled loudly and exclaimed with a big smile, "I did it!" Heading back to the highway, instead of turning back toward home, she followed the sign that pointed to Denver. Stone-faced again, she didn't say another word.

We parked in front of a shabby apartment house, climbed four flights of stairs, then went through a planked door and up a narrow set of steps into the attic. Marilyn stood there, caught unawares. She stared at us, her face furrowed and stressed. I couldn't move, filled with shock and confusion. What was happening? When I saw Ellin some time ago, I thought Marilyn might also be alive, but I wasn't sure. Daddy had always gotten the angriest at her. She could have been killed while Ellin somehow escaped. So many nights I had lain awake agonizing.

A cry interrupted my thoughts and I jolted to the presence of a baby in the room—no, two! Marilyn glanced only briefly at me while she and Mother stood talking in terse tones. I walked over to the babies, ducking to keep from hitting my head on the splintery rafters that slanted low toward the wall. An infant lay on a blanket in a cardboard box on the bare floor. A little boy not much more than a year old, his dirty thumb in his mouth, stood nearby staring at me. In spite of the chilly, unheated room, they both wore only stained undershirts and soggy diapers. A bucket overflowing with diapers stunk by the sink, heaped with dirty dishes and rotting food. My stomach convulsed and for moments I thought I might throw up.

We stayed only for a few hours, none of this time in the apartment. Marilyn changed the babies' diapers and wrapped both of them in blankets, and we piled into the car, the four of them in front while I sat alone in back. Mother stopped at a service station to fill up with gas and, when she went in to pay, came out with two bottles of beer. She handed them to Marilyn to hold, then parked at the far side of the station so they could drink them. As Mother reached for her beer, she commented contemptuously to Marilyn (loudly so I could hear), that I "was probably disapproving back there, since I was all Newsom." Marilyn tipped her beer and guzzled, then over her shoulder, in a superior tone, told me beer was good for a nursing mother. Ignoring me, they talked earnestly in low tones, words I couldn't hear. I stared out the window, feeling miserable. That accusation by Mother again: "all Newsom." Neither of them wanted me here. Why was I here?

At a grocery store the two of them pushed the basket around and heaped it with baby food, boxes and cans, and a large package of hamburger. Marilyn looked tearful as she put that in the basket, telling Mother it was her first meat in months. I tagged along behind.

Back at the apartment building, Mother loaded me with grocery sacks and gathered more, while Marilyn carried the children. We trudged up the stairs to the attic and put all the sacks on the floor; Mother sent me back to the car to carry up the rest. When everything was stacked against a wall, Mother handed Marilyn some money, but told her she couldn't do any more. Marilyn had gotten herself into this mess and she would have to get herself out.

Her words recalled that time years ago when Marilyn brought home a stray puppy, an adorable eager little fluff she had found abandoned and hungry. She put out a dish of water and some food, and after supper we all went to the movies, a special and rare event for our family. We returned to the stink of big pools of diarrhea all over the two rooms of our house. Mother smirked at Marilyn and told her that since she had wanted the puppy, now she could clean this up. She and Daddy went into their room and closed the door.

Marilyn looked at the mess and burst into hysterical tears. Grabbing the sick puppy, she opened the back door and, screaming, hurled it out into the darkness. We never saw it again.

Now, without a hug or a soft word, Mother turned and descended the stairs. I stood looking back and forth at both of them, then followed Mother. I looked back the final time as I heard Marilyn start to sob. Both babies were screaming. Everything felt horribly wrong. I started to say something in the car, but Mother looked straight ahead and headed back to the highway, ignoring me and my tears.

Filled with pain and a rising anger, I felt the same bewilderment as I had when we went to see Ellin. It was the same all over again. The only time Mother even acknowledged my presence on this trip was when she made that scornful comment about me to Marilyn. Now she ignored me the entire long, silent trip home. After we arrived, Daddy asked Mother if we had had a good time. She responded triumphantly that she had driven to the top of Pike's Peak. She never mentioned Marilyn. Did he know we had gone to see her? Did he even know about her and her two babies? We settled into our usual silence.

Thirteen years old by then, I had been babysitting several evenings a week for more than a year. I earned fifteen cents an hour, and paid my own expenses, which were few. Mostly I did without. While in Denver I copied Marilyn's address on the edge of a paper scrap, and after we returned home, I took on extra jobs and sent her half of everything I earned. Months later, she wrote a brief note to thank me, telling me that I had kept her in hamburger.

New Beginnings

ℰ

Mr. Crandall, our new junior-high-school principal, moved to town that summer. A professional yet still new to our community, he chose a house in the valley on Walnut Street, two blocks from my family. He and his wife Mary hired me to babysit their three preschool-age daughters. Gradually Mary asked me to help her with the laundry and other household chores. On hot days, she squeezed fresh lemons and we sat on the front porch steps, hoping to catch a breeze, drinking lemonade in ice-cube-filled glasses that we rubbed against our faces and necks. On the most sultry days, she packed a picnic supper for a cook-out at the lake, and they always invited me. The little girls squabbled over who would sit beside me in the back seat of their car. With them I felt the warmth of belonging.

One July evening, while on a picnic with them, I developed a piercing stomachache that worsened before they could get me to a doctor. He determined my appendix was about to burst and rushed me into surgery. When he had difficulty finding my appendix, he had to keep extending the incision. Then complications developed. Later he told my parents they were lucky to still have me.

During those two miserable weeks I was recovering in the hot hospital room, I can't remember my parents visiting. Since I was the only patient in the hospital, Vera the nurse kept me company every afternoon, sitting in front of my window. She had a fan for each of us. Their bold black letters read: "Compliments of Thompson's Funeral Home." Vera told me stories about her nursing experiences, about her children, and about the things she did when she was my age. Once she told me, "One day you'll have a baby, but that pain will be nothing compared to what you suffered with this."

The hospital was located above shops on Main Street, and we amused ourselves by peering down into the cars of people who parked below. We chuckled watching the women squirm as they struggled to pull up nylon stockings flumped around their ankles, attaching them to their garter belts before getting out of their cars. Once out, they'd tug at their skirts, and, looking back, pull at their stockings to make sure their seams were straight. Even in the Kansas summer heat, every woman who lived on the hill dressed in nylons and high heels to go to town.

ഢ ഢ ഢ

The day Mother took me home, she and Vera edged me down the long flight of stairs from the hospital into our car, an excruciating descent for me. As we drove, Mother said she and Daddy were leaving the next day to drive to California with a couple who worked at the wholesale floral market in Wichita. That couple invited them to go, and the two couples would split the cost of the trip. Mother said the business was stagnant in this heat, and I was only going to be recovering, so they might as well go. They had arranged for Iva, a florist in a nearby town, to stay during their absence. Iva was the wife of Carl, a friend of Daddy's in high school and college. The two young men had worked at a floral shop on Saturdays together and remained distant but firm friends all these years. Iva could cover the business if a funeral should come up and could drive me to the doctor's office when it was time to take out my stitches. Mother put a cot under the walnut tree in the front yard for me, and a chair beside it where Iva could sit, cooler for both of us she said. Then Mother and Daddy left.

I knew Iva only slightly, and staying alone with her remained uncomfortably strained. I lay silently on my cot during those long hot days, while Iva sat in a chair beside me, fanning herself with a newspaper. She was kind to me and ready to help, but she and Carl had never had children and she seemed just as uncomfortable with me. I felt shy to ask for anything, embarrassed when needing her help to walk into the house for the bathroom, and reluctant to tell her when I was thirsty or hungry. I wished she would go to the library and get me some books, but I couldn't ask for that, either. I thought she had to stay for the business anyway, in case a customer came. The hours dragged by. I spent my days staring up at the leaves of the tree, watching two squirrels scurry around harvesting the black walnuts and burying them in the yard.

When Mother and Daddy returned a week later—a week earlier than planned—they were in a bad mood. Mother said the trip had been terrible. No one had had anything to say to each other after the first ten miles in that hot car, and they discovered they shared not one thing in common as to what they hoped to see or do in California. By mutual agreement, after less than one day there, they turned around and drove home in stony silence. "We might just as well have stayed home with you," she added.

～ ～ ～

By the time school started the week after Labor Day, I had recovered sufficiently to attend, though I had to remain at my desk during recess. Mr. Crandall assumed his role as both principal of the school and teacher of our eighth-grade class, and my experience with school began to improve dramatically from the previous year. I still stung with the pain of those humiliating experiences. When he joined the Presbyterian Church, he became my Sunday school teacher and my eighth-grade teacher, as well, and I continued to babysit for his family. All of this provided an important support for me. I had needed an adult, one who was respected in our community, to believe in me and stand by me. This I found in Mr. Crandall.

Mr. Crandall required each of us to memorize a poem every week and recite it in front of the class. I was terrified to perform. The first time I stood up, I mumbled the words and rushed back to my seat. Mr. Crandall called me back with a kind smile and asked me to face him, my back to the class. He praised my having memorized the poem so well and asked me to repeat it, only to him this time. I could speak as softly as I wished. When I finished, he turned to the class, complimented me, and paraphrased Matthew 5:14-16: "Let your light shine before others—don't hide your lamp under a basket—let people see your good works." When he told the class that my light was shining that day, they applauded. I looked around, surprised.

Mr. Crandall wanted us to grow strong characters and would frequently quote sayings of famous people. He especially admired Robert Burns, and often repeated his admonition: "You can fool all of the people some of the time, and some of the people all the time, but you can never fool all the people all the time." He usually quoted this when one of us was caught trying to get away with something.

Every week I practiced hard on my poem. Mr. Crandall always found something to praise in my recitation, frequently telling me my lamp was shining brightly that day. Some of my classmates became friendlier. My flickering courage grew stronger. Although my fears never went away completely, gradually I stopped being so afraid of school, even began to make a few friends.

Before I entered high school that autumn, however, someone else moved to our town who would influence my life even more than the Crandalls.

~ ~ ~

Lorraine and her husband bought the Farmer's and Drover's National Bank, a prestigious ownership, and moved to Marion that summer. Their one daughter was away at college. They moved into a comfortable home on the hill and were quickly embraced into the community. They also joined the Presbyterian Church, and soon Lorraine, a former schoolteacher, agreed to take over our Sunday school class from Mr. Crandall, because of his time pressures. Lorraine's warmth brought a whole new enthusiasm that inspired our interest, a spirit that bubbled over outside that one hour on Sunday.

She and a friend (an avid tennis player) invited the four of us in her Sunday school class to the park's tennis courts to teach us the basics of tennis. We met once a week, and after two hours smacking balls around the cracked cement, we sat beside the fountain to share the snacks Lorraine had packed. When she and her husband bought a cabin at the nearby lake, they invited us there every Sunday night for wiener roasts, to toast marshmallows and sing campfire songs as we watched the sun set into the water. At Easter, we rose in the dark to be at the lake for a sunrise service and special breakfast. Each of us felt how much Lorraine enjoyed and genuinely cared about us.

Through a state-level officer of the church who contacted our minister, we learned that—unknown to us—Lorraine had risen to hold offices in the Presbyterian Church at large, first on the state level, and then she had been elected and was the first woman to serve as a Director on the National Board. She flew once a month to New York City for their meetings, though she never mentioned any of this. She told me once that if anything she did was of any importance, it would become apparent through her actions, not her words. Liked by everyone who met her, Lorraine emerged as the most revered woman in town.

One Sunday, Lorraine invited me to her house for tea the following Wednesday afternoon. These Wednesday get-togethers became our weekly special time. After I helped her prepare the tea in her kitchen, we carried the tray into the sitting room and settled across from each other in the matching easy chairs, in front of a large picture window that overlooked her English flower garden— an expansive display she developed that was featured in the annual city garden tour each summer.

We sipped tea from her Wedgwood cups with pink roses and munched her homemade cookies. She had grown up on a farm in a poor family and went to school barefoot when they couldn't afford shoes. She spoke of this only once to me, with no self-pity, but shared it to explain how she realized their poverty had toughened her and been the root of her commitment to education. Through persistence she had attended college to get her teaching degree, and for years tried to inspire young people to rise above any obstacles to follow their dreams. Some days she pulled out one of her well-thumbed inspirational books to read portions to me, and every birthday and Christmas she gave me a book for my own. I became both her special friend and protégé.

An attractive woman, to me Lorraine was everything my Mother wasn't. She enjoyed people and conversed easily, dressed tastefully, had warm, gracious manners and entertained often in her refined, comfortable home. Women dropped by frequently to talk with her, knowing she would listen, and when they needed a shoulder to cry on, she was always a voice of encouragement. At last I had a role model for the kind of woman I wanted to be, and this woman had confidence that I had potential.

Because of Lorainne's friendship and support of me, the rest of the church members (all hill families) began to pay attention to me in a new light. Though some were a bit reserved at first, eventually their acceptance of me became wholehearted. A small group of women leaders in our church became a strong support as I stumbled through my adolescent years, just as some of the women in my neighborhood had been during my earlier years.

Lorraine and her husband remained cordial to my parents, but they shared nothing in common. Once, when Lorraine stopped to talk with Mother and me after church, Mother smirked and made one of her derogatory comments about me. When Lorraine didn't laugh, or even seem puzzled (as most people did), but simply stood there and looked at her, Mother sobered, turned and walked quickly to our car. Once, sounding hurt, Mother complained I spent all my time at Lorraine's house. Surprised that she noticed or even cared, I decided I would spend more time with Mother. That lasted for one afternoon. It only confirmed that neither of us knew what to say or do together. Most of the time I thought Mother seemed relieved that I had that relationship with Lorraine, as though it took the responsibility off her shoulders. But I sensed Mother's confusion, perhaps even surprise, when I saw her watching Lorraine and me together.

Even though I knew that my family's reputation made no difference to Lorraine in our relationship, and even though she remained my unshakable friend and never once let me down, nothing eased my fear that I might blunder and do something wrong that would ruin her faith in me. I worked hard to be what

I thought she wanted me to be and remained guarded about what I shared during our times together. I never talked about my family or anything that went on in our home. I couldn't risk losing her friendship.

With Mr. Crandall's and Lorraine's support and faith in me, I entered high school with a growing confidence and began to open to the pleasures of school. First one girl, and then another, invited me to her home. Slowly I became part of a circle of friends from both the hill and the valley. Some hill families still would not have anything to do with me, but I remained friendly while mostly ignoring them. The new positives in my life began to eclipse those familiar old snubs.

~ ~ ~

As our class prepared that summer for our freshman year in senior high school, all of us had to cope with our first challenge. On our final day of junior high, Mr. Crandall told us to each write a book report during the summer that we would give to our senior high school English teacher during our first class in September. We had never done book reports, and he explained how we should work from an outline: write the title, author, summary of the story, and tell whether we liked it or not, and why.

For years, I had loved long hours in the library. Mrs. Ray, our librarian, always welcomed me and never seemed to mind when I sprawled out on the floor in the children's section. I read for hours in front of the fan, the air sweeping back and forth across my face ruffling my hair. As I grew older, occasionally she would walk over to me with a new book, pat my shoulder as she handed it to me, and tell me I was the first one to open it. Before I turned a page, for long moments I absorbed the feel of it and traced the lettering and figures on the cover. I pressed it to my face to breathe in its smell, different from the older books on the shelves. Even the pages felt smooth and clean, with no crinkles or turned-down corners or finger smudges. To me, a book was a kind of miracle, all these pages covered with squiggles that we learned how to decipher to unlock the book's story.

Sinking into a story, I imagined myself becoming the various characters, trying on each identity to discover whether it fit. My name remained a constant reminder to me of how Mother was flooded with despair when I wasn't born a Robert and of all the pain that continued between her and me. She hadn't felt better in the hospital when Daddy patted her arm and said: "It's all right. We'll just add an a." I wished I could change my name—if only in my imagination.

For a while I became the orphan, Ann, or rather "Anne with an e" in *Anne of Green Gables*. I loved her spunk. She lived on a farm on a beautiful island with an elderly, unmarried brother and sister. And even though she wasn't the boy they had expected to adopt from the orphanage, they kept her and grew to love her. She met a girl who became her bosom friend.

I understood why Anne wanted to be called Cordelia when she arrived at Green Gables, even though she only succeeded in adding an "e" to her plain name of Ann. She wanted to shed her old life, that life of loneliness, where no one had wanted her.

Still, the name Anne didn't seem to suit me. It sounded too short—like Jo, in *Little Women*. I liked the spunk of this character, too. Had her mother hoped for a Joe? That mother never had a son either, yet she loved all four of her girls. I decided I liked this family and imagined myself belonging there. But I would lengthen the name Jo. I became Joanna.

Now, with Mr. Crandall's assignment, I wandered through the library trying to choose the right book. Nothing. Finally, I decided to ask Mrs. Ray for suggestions. She handed me a new book the library had just received: *Enchanting Jenny Lind* by Laura Benet. I signed the checkout card from the envelope pasted inside the back cover and watched her file it in her red recipe box with the picture of an apple pie on its lid. I carried the book to my favorite spot in front of the fan, lay down on the floor and studied it, then began reading.

The similarities of Jenny Lind and myself startled me. Both of us had birthdays in October, and when the story opened, she was thirteen too, like me. She was born and lived in Sweden; my Grandma Larson was born and raised in Sweden. And Jenny Lind's real name was Johanna, the European version of Joanna.

Johanna also was a lonely girl. She lived with her mother and grandmother. While her mother worked to pay for their meager existence, her grandmother grudgingly cared for Johanna, remaining cold and critical, like Grandma Larson when she had been forced to take care of me. Her exhausted mother returned each night wanting to be left alone, telling Johanna how much easier things would have been if only she had never been born, words all too familiar to me.

The parallels continued. Shunned by her peers, she escaped to the woods to play alone, as I did for years at Dogfish Island. She loved the birds and amused herself by singing to imitate them. One day, a music teacher walking in the woods overheard her and convinced her mother to allow Johanna to study with him every day at his studio. She worked hard and eventually became famous, changed her first name to Jenny, and became known as the Swedish Nightingale. She won the hearts of people internationally, including the Queen of England when she sang at Buckingham Palace.

I devoured this book, believing I had found someone just like me, except she had been born with that gorgeous voice. I sang in the church choir and enjoyed singing, but my voice couldn't compare, and my miserable failure singing the lead in our seventh-grade school play still hurt. I could never become a Swedish nightingale and perform for the Queen. Still, in all other ways, I identified deeply with Johanna, and decided to write about her story for my book report.

Early the next morning, I shut the windows in our living room and pulled down the water-stained brown shades, hoping to trap the night's coolness. I hated the closed-in feeling and the dim light, but when the heat and humidity rose, our house still stunk like Mud Creek that had flooded our valley several years before. While I was safely on the hill, my parents had hosed out the rooms as the flood water receded, trying to get the slime out of our house, but they never could get rid of the residue deep within crevices in the warped boards. The stench returned on rainy days, or whenever the temperature increased, and the air thickened with humidity.

I unfolded the old card table and set it up in the middle of the room. After the flood, Mother had replaced the soggy top with a piece of plywood. I spread my project on this, propping the book so that Jenny Lind's face on the cover looked into my eyes. To soften the splintery surface, I placed extra sheets of lined notebook paper on the plywood, then filled my pen from the bottle of Script's blue-black ink.

I stared into Jenny Lind's face. How could I begin to capture onto a piece of paper all that filled my heart as I read her story? Following the guidelines Mr. Crandall had given us, I wrote the title, then the author. Next was the summary. I sat. My sweaty arms stuck to the paper. I sat some more, then began moving my pen across the page.

"As a child, Jenny Lind didn't have a happy home." The dimness of the room disappeared. I no longer smelled the mustiness or noticed the humidity. The shaky table lent itself to the paper, and my pen began to glide. One page, two, then three. I finished with the words: "I liked this story. I met a girl who had a life very much like mine. If we had grown up together, we would have become bosom friends. Through her singing she found a place where she belonged and became happy. Even though I don't have a voice like hers, her story gives me hope that if I want something with all my heart and work hard, I will find my place too."

I put down my pen. I read my three pages filled with blue words. Where had they come from? As I stared at them, they began to blur, expanding beyond my page, beyond this room, like a huge sky opening and beckoning to me. I looked at Jenny Lind's face, framed by singing nightingales, and imagined those birds becoming her voice, soaring across this blue blue sky. On the wings of my words, I had risen too—flying free above my home, my neighborhood, even the town. When the blue on my pages settled once again into words, something was different.

Writing that report had given me my first glimpse into something that made my heart sing. I built myself a desk in front of the window in my bedroom that overlooked the old mulberry tree. Mr. Schmersey at the grocery store gave me two orange crates, and on Daddy's wood pile I found a thin wooden box that had been used for shipping panes of glass for the greenhouses. It was the perfect size, its thickness five inches, with one length-long side open. I set this box on top of the two crates, with space in the middle for a chair. At the dime store, I bought a large desk blotter, and thumbtacked it for a smooth top. I finished by tacking chicken feed sacks (the ones with wildflowers designed on the fabric) around the edges of the crates. In the open side of the desk box, I had room for a shallow cardboard box to hold my pencils, pens and erasure, and I slid my Red Chief tablets beside it. The inside of the orange crates provided shelves hidden by the feed-sack curtain for my books and treasures. I took the lamp from my parent's dust-covered desk. They didn't seem to notice, as Mother did all their business at the desk in the greenhouse office. In the corner on the top of my desk, I put one of Mother's jelly jars and I would fill it with clover blossoms from the alfalfa field. Once I discovered a four-leafed one that I believed brought good luck. I loved my desk, even the smell of the wood, and I spent hours there studying and writing assignments.

During my junior year, when I elected to take a typing class, I found a Royal portable typewriter on my desk. Mother bought it for me from the county newspaper office that sold these. She told me every girl should learn typing and shorthand so she could always get a job. I fell in love with my typewriter and clattered away on it every night. By the end of that semester, our typing instructor told me that my speed of ninety-five words per minute with accuracy qualified me to apply as a court reporter. Mother glowed. Although I loved typing, being a court reporter didn't interest me.

My favorite assignments were writing papers for our English classes. These were few, but I kept each one in a folder on one of my crate shelves. Although my teachers wrote positive remarks on my papers, no one encouraged me to work on my writing. Even during moments when I filled with awe, moments when I experienced words emerging from some unknown place inside me to evolve into something magical, it didn't occur to me that I could pursue writing as something other than a way to fulfill my assignments. Instead, clarinet became my passion.

In fourth grade, I was handed this instrument by the teacher who was forming a band. During high school I grew serious, took lessons at a nearby college from a prestigious teacher, and beginning at 5:00 a.m. practiced four hours every day, two hours before school and two hours after. With my hard work I excelled and was awarded a college music scholarship.

However, having grown up in my troubled family, experiencing the violence toward my sisters, I was gripped by a certainty that, in the future, I had to be doing something to help children who suffered like them. How else could I deal with my guilt, the one responsible for their misery, but to search for some Divine message and guidance in it all? I served two summers in our church mission programs for needy children, that resulted both in my becoming highly respected in our church and Lorraine becoming enthusiastic that she had successfully guided her young protégé.

My bondage to this commitment strengthened, I believed I was following God's will for my life and threw myself into it wholeheartedly. I wasn't free to listen to my own heart and explore the other possibilities open to me, regardless of how magnetic those options were.

It would take decades for me to understand I had chosen this path for all the wrong reasons. Although I performed well in my profession of clinical social work, working with families or individuals suffering from abuse, for which I had deep understanding and compassion, it never fulfilled my heart.

Gentle Touches

That next spring, red posters appeared in shop windows caus- ing a buzz to ripple through our town. A rodeo was launching its spring tour here. Usually this happened in Strong City, thirty miles east of us, considered the rodeo capital of the world. When I was nine, Daddy took me to one there. Cowboys competed for who could stay the longest on a wildly bucking horse. A strap pulled painfully around its groin caused it to buck. Next came the calf-roping contest. A calf released from a pen ran frantically around the arena while a cowboy raced his horse after it, roped and threw it hard to the ground, then leaped from his saddle and tied its legs together. While the calf writhed, eyes wide with terror, the cowboy sprang up, pumping his fists triumphantly, the crowd screaming with excitement. I burst into tears with the third calf. Daddy took my hand and led me to our car. Five years later that experience still remained etched into my memory.

To me, a rodeo was just a heartless event for cowboys to show off. Their Quarter horses might be efficient cow ponies, the horse and rider dazzling in their glittering dress, but it made me feel sick. I wanted to get away from bullying and cruelty. My secret yearning was not for a rodeo where cowboys swaggered, but to see the really great horses, the thoroughbreds in Kentucky. I had yet to learn the cruelty of horse racing.

I learned everything I could about Kentucky's horse farms, read every book in the library, checked the magazines each month as they appeared on the drug store racks. Occasionally, I overheard a customer chuckle to my parents that I was "horse-crazy," but no one really knew. I wasn't crazy about just any horse. In my fantasies, I owned the finest horse in the whole world, the magnificent though fictional Arabian stallion Shatan, from my favorite book, *The Black Stallion*. On my way home from school, certain no one was watching, I would lean forward in the stirrups to press against Shatan's long neck, clutch the reins, and feel his muscles churn beneath my legs. I talked low into his ear, urging him on, feeling him surge faster and faster, responding out of love for me, straining with everything he had, racing his heart out on this grand racetrack, then dashing across the finish line lengths ahead of all the other thoroughbreds. Sweaty and exhilarated, I bounded up the back-porch steps of our house and slid off his back, wrapping my arms around his glistening neck. "We did it, boy, we did it!"

When a magazine came out with the history of the Kentucky Derby, featuring its all-time-champion Man-o-War, every day after school I stopped at the Rexall drugstore to sit cross-legged on the floor by the magazine rack and devour the photos. It showed Man-o-War's home, Calumet Farm in Lexington, Kentucky, and the nearby horse farms—vast emerald fields, huge white horse barns, and miles of gleaming white fences. Throughout our Kansas countryside, the farms usually had faded red barns, and fences of barbed wire nailed to tilting posts that enclosed fields too often dusty and brown. I dreamed of visiting these Kentucky horse farms, where I'd lean against a white fence and watch thoroughbreds graze in their lush green fields, walk through barns immaculately kept, and see champions in their stalls munching oats or being rubbed down by handlers, maybe I'd even go to the Derby and watch these champions thunder around the track. I dreamed of standing beside Man-o-War's stall, seeing him in all his magnificence, reaching up and rubbing his muzzle. I wasn't interested in watching cow ponies chase helpless calves on a dusty football field. Just once, I wanted to feel the touch of greatness.

Three days before the rodeo, as we clustered around our lockers in the school hallway, some boys sidled near me talking loudly. "Hey, man," Bob said, "do you guys know this isn't just a rodeo? It's a real horse show. Class, man, class."

Maurice drew closer, speaking in a low, confidential voice. "Did ya' know they're bringing in real Arabian horses? No kidding. They're flying 'em over."

My heart began to pound. I drew closer to them. "Really?"

The boys looked surprised I had overheard them. "Yeah, honest. And not just for here. The show then moves on east, all the way to Madison Square Garden. It's a big deal."

"Yeah man, but I'm POed," Bob said. "Five bucks a ticket. I hope my dad will help me out."

I stopped, my excitement crushed. There was no way I could afford a five-dollar ticket. Yet—a real horse show, with champions. Obsessed, all morning I thought of nothing else but this show that was coming right here to our small town. I approached my classmate, Mary Jo. She didn't have much money either and might want to go. When I told her the details about the show, she grew excited too, but gasped at the ticket price. We had to find a way to go.

By the end of the day, I had an idea. We could sneak in. The show opened Saturday night. It would be dark. If we walked out the main road to the cut-off, we would be half a mile from the athletic field where the show would be held. We could cross the adjoining pasture and enter the back way. No one would see us. It might work. We began to make our plans.

That Saturday, as evening dusk deepened, Mary Jo and I started out. Whenever we saw a car, we dove into the ditch and flipped off our flashlights. As we entered the pasture, since we could see people across the field at the event, we were afraid they could see us too, so we left our flashlights off. We couldn't take any chances. And, as we drew closer, we'd have to crawl across the field, very low to the ground. We couldn't risk walking upright.

We squirmed forward on our stomachs, inching across the ground, our eyes straining to adjust to the blackness of this moonless night. Thistles pierced our skin. Grass rustled near us. Was that a snake? We crawled faster. "Ewwee! Yuck!" Mary Jo exclaimed. "Cow pie." She tried to wipe her hand clean on the stubble.

Clouds of dust billowed in the light of the athletic field. Voices drifted from the loudspeaker. Giddy with anticipation we cheered each other on. "We're so close. We can make it!" We remained flat on the ground as we approached the fence, checking that no one was near, then took turns lifting the strands of barbed wire while the other wriggled under. "We made it!" we exclaimed, hugging each other.

Suddenly the headlights of a car drove straight toward us, freezing us in their glare. Tires spit gravel as the car skidded to a stop. The sheriff and his deputy leaped out and strode toward us, holsters bumping against their legs.

"Well—well—well now, did you boys really think you could pull a fast one on us?" drawled the Sheriff. He looked closer. "Oh-my-God-almighty. They're girls!" The two men shone their flashlights up and down each of us. "What on the Lord's good earth do you girls think you're doing? If you aren't the sorriest lookin' sight I've ever seen," said the sheriff.

We stood in their spotlight, hanging our heads, plastered with sweat, dust and cow dung, our skin throbbing from stickle-burrs and thistles. The sheriff paused, then stepped forward to shine his light full in my face. "Roberta Newsom? Is that you?"

I couldn't look at him, desperately wanting to disappear right into the ground, but began babbling: "I'm sorry I'm so sorry I wanted to see the horse show so much but couldn't afford to pay $5.00 and thought we could get in this way and I talked Mary Jo into this it's all my idea it's all my fault I'm really really sorry ..."

"Five dollars!" the sheriff snorted, interrupting me. "What are you talkin' about? Didn't you girls know student tickets cost thirty-five cents?"

I stammered, confused. He chuckled grimly. "I think some-one's been pullin' yer leg." He jerked the back door open to his car. "Come on. Get in," he ordered.

The two men slid into the front seat. The sheriff turned toward his deputy and asked gruffly, "Do you think we should lock 'em up?" The deputy grunted and turned to look out his window. Silently the men drove us to our homes. Would they tell our parents? They went first to Mary Jo's house. When they stopped in front of mine, the sheriff turned around and said sternly, "Get cleaned up. We'll be back in forty-five minutes. Be ready." They sped off.

The radio was on in our dim living room. I crept up the stairs and closed myself into the bathroom, peeled off my clothes and inched into the tub. I turned on the water, only a trickle, holding my breath the pipes wouldn't rattle, and began sponging off the cow dung, pushing bits down the drain. It stunk even worse when it got wet. I tweezed out the largest of the thorns and stickers, then dabbed iodine on the raw places, the dark maroon splotching my arms and legs.

Breaking into a sweat, suddenly I became faint. The sheriff would take us to jail. We'd miss school and the whole town would know. We'd have to pay a fine before they'd release us, so we'd sit in that cell maybe forever. I thought of Mary Jo's mother, who was always friendly. She wouldn't want me in her home anymore. No one would ever trust me now. I would lose my jobs, so I couldn't send money to Marilyn. I had gotten one job at the movie theater to operate the popcorn machine on Saturdays, and two months ago the manager gave me a key to lock up at night after I cleaned the greasy popcorn machine and swept the lobby floor. And I was increasingly asked to babysit. The wife of a prominent lawyer, a hill family, recently left me with her three-week-old baby along with her two pre-school boys. She said it was a lot, but she knew I was responsible.

My sweat turned icy and I couldn't stop shivering. The full weight of what I had done hit me. I had worked so hard for so long, and at last I was establishing my own reputation in our com-munity—that of a girl who was reliable and could be trusted. Now I had betrayed both myself and those who had begun to believe in me. My head ached. Sick with regret, I realized I couldn't wish away the consequences, regardless of how sorry I felt.

I waited on the front porch, my teeth chattering, clutching a paper sack containing my toothbrush, tooth powder, and clean underpants. Mary Jo was already in the sheriff's car. She and I huddled together gripping each other's hands, sinking low into the back seat hoping no one could see us. The men turned down the street toward the jail, slowed the car as we approached... slower... slower... but then sped up.

The sheriff waved his hand to the ticket-takers at the gate as he drove through. He stopped the car out of sight and opened the car door for us. I slid across the seat, holding my paper bag carefully, afraid it might split. The four of us stood beside the car, hearing the roar from the grandstand. "I could talk to you both," he said, "but then, I don't think I need to. And no one besides the four of us ever needs to know anything about this. You girls go on in and enjoy the rodeo."

Stunned with disbelief, I tried to mumble thank you, but when my frozen lips couldn't form words, I burst into tears. The sheriff looked at me, his eyes soft, and placed his hand gently on my shoulder. Then he turned, and with his deputy, climbed into their car and drove away.

Mary Jo and I cried and hugged until I began hiccupping, which made us laugh. Wiping our faces, we lied, reassuring each other we looked fine. Approaching the bleachers, we sniffed ourselves. In spite of our scrubbing, we still stunk, but we hoped people would think it was the horses. We climbed up and sat on a hard plank.

We never saw an Arabian horse. Cowboys raced their Quarter Horses around barrels up and down the field, creating swirls of dust. Next would be the competition to lasso the calves. Men were bringing them from pens behind the stands, releasing them one-by-one onto the field. They blinked in the bright lights, their eyes large and wild, their spindly legs trembling. Mary Jo and I looked at each other, then without a word, slipped out of our seats. We limped across the grounds and out the gate to begin our long walk home.

ᴗ ᴗ ᴗ

During supper one evening that July, my parents told me we were going to take our first vacation. Business had been good, they had saved a bit of money, and now the greenhouses would go dormant in the August heat. Daddy set a shoebox on the table. "We've got cold cash," he said with a silly grin, delighted with his joke. They had kept this box in the floral cooler since last January, and at the end of every day tossed in their loose change. He hefted it up, proud of its weight.

For the first time since buying the greenhouse, this year they had made a tiny profit. Mother said that, to celebrate, we would take a road trip to Kentucky, first to see Stephen Foster's home, and then to go to Lexington to visit some horse farms. I listened to them, dumbfounded. Daddy decided he would get the tires checked on the car and replace that thin one if necessary, while Mother thought about home-canned jars of fruits and vegetables in our basement we could take for our meals. There was a lightness edged with anticipation in their voices.

After supper, I climbed the ladder to my perch in the black walnut tree to think. I had been aware something was changing in our house. My parents' faces weren't tense all the time, their voices less worried sounding when they talked about the business. Making a profit this year had eased things for them, but it was something more. Since my sisters left, even though we still ate our meals mostly in silence, the silence itself felt different. We weren't tensely on edge, as Daddy no longer exploded into unexpected violence. I still worried about my sisters. Mother had never mentioned either of them since we made those trips to see them. I had learned they were alive, though they might as well be dead, the way everyone acted as though they didn't even exist.

I didn't tell anyone I had sent money to Marilyn. Aside from that one thank-you, I hadn't heard from her. Several weeks later, my envelope with my money for that month was returned. She had moved and left no forwarding address. I wondered where she was and whether she and the babies were all right. Did Mother know she moved, and where she had gone? Their absence had made things better for us, though I still resented that no one explained to me what had happened. And now, why would my parents decide to go on a vacation to the very places I most wanted to see?

What I didn't grasp was that—as I gradually excelled and became respected and accepted in our community—my parents benefitted from this as well. Even though they still had no friends, many people were friendlier to them and chatted when they came to the floral shop. My sisters were no longer around, and, although I never understood why they had not been liked in the community, my efforts to be accepted seemed to separate me from them, and even helped fade their memories, which reflected well on my parents. In me, also, my parents had something beside their work to share. They had never taken a vacation together because, without a single mutual interest, they would not have known where to go. My passion now gave them a destination for a vacation; my presence served as a buffer. I had become special to them.

Everything was so complicated and confusing. Just the day before, I overheard a customer say to Mother, "You must be so proud of Roberta. She's such a responsible girl."

"Yes," Mother replied. "She's my only daughter who has never given me one moment of trouble."

This startled me. Was she beginning to accept me, perhaps just a little bit? Shifting more comfortably against a limb, I remembered the pair of panties and half-slip with appliqued hearts that I found on my bed last Valentine's Day. Satiny and soft, I held them against my cheek, smelling their faint, sweet perfume. I went to the greenhouse and asked Mother about them. Not looking at me, she said offhandedly, "Oh, I delivered some bouquets to the opening of Van's dress shop and thought I should buy something."

Daddy always made the deliveries; Mother seldom went to town. I wanted her to tell me she took the flowers so she could browse in the new shop and look for a love gift for me. But it was probably as she said. She simply wanted to check out the new (and only) women's dress shop in town and thought she'd better buy something, so the owner would buy from us. Mother never bought anything for herself; by default, I was the only one she had that she could buy something for. I walked away, not telling her how much I loved the underwear.

There were other unexpected things that appeared in my room, each one feminine and dainty, such as a ceramic girl with flowing hair and long dress, her face tilted toward the flowers she held. And a lovely miniature pendant, a pastoral scene hand-painted by a gifted lady artist in town. Mother bought both of these at the art fair held in the city park the prior summer.

I lay back along the branch, staring at the sky through the leaves, and remembered my autograph book. In eighth grade, each of the girls in my class bought one at the dime store and everyone signed each other's. Feeling a touch of ambivalence, wondering if she would even sign it and if so, what she'd say, I asked Mother to write in mine. When she gave it back several days later, I hurried to my room, heart pounding, and flipped through pages of "Roses are red" clichés. Then I found the page with her handwriting using Shakespeare's words:

"This above all: to thine own self be true,
And it must follow, as the night the day,
Thou canst not then be false to any man."
Love,

Mother

I stared at her writing, my face hot, filling with a strange confusion. Mother had paid for me to join the Shakespeare class on Saturday mornings offered by Mrs. Matlock, our local elderly Grand Dame trained in the classics. She must have been looking through my textbook and saw that passage I marked with red pencil. The lines spoke to my heart as I read them, although their meaning would take a lifetime to understand and try to live. Mother, too, had thought them special, or at least saw they were special to me. Was she interested in seeing what I was learning, or perhaps wanted to learn about Shakespeare herself? Suddenly I felt incensed, as though she had invaded something very personal of mine. But then I felt ashamed. Why did this offend me? She had put thought and effort into deciding what to write. Maybe she had struggled and searched for something to say, wanting it to be special. I couldn't admit even to myself how much I wanted to be special to her, how much I wanted us to have a close relationship, how much I wanted her to write heartfelt words of her own in my book.

But the hurt had been too deep for too long between Mother and me. It never occurred to me that—not understanding—I now froze her out of my life, coldly refusing her attempts to be closer. With her, I remained on guard, always apprehensive, ultra-sensitive to the occasional scathing accusations she still unleashed at me. They hurt. I never could relax with her, regardless of her gifts. I hardened, resenting customer being friendly to her, resenting that Mother might be finding acceptance in our community through my own years of efforts. I thought it sweet revenge that I didn't need her, but now she needed me—even copied me.

The limb grew sharp against my back and I shifted. I loved that Shakespeare class. I knew Mother didn't have much money, yet she had found a way to give this to me. Years before, she bought a set of World Books from a traveling salesman for us girls, mailing the twenty-five-cents payment every month. She also had scraped together money to buy an old upright piano that we somehow squeezed into our cramped living area. Marilyn and Ellin both had excellent voices and spent hours together at the piano, dreaming they were going to be famous pop singers, or better yet, write songs that would become hits and make millions of dollars. They wrote score after score of songs, playing and singing them together to hear if they worked. I listened to them while curled up on the couch with a volume of the World Book.

I began hearing words in my head—of a poem. Where did they come from? I felt strangely frightened, yet strained to remember. "O the Raggedy man—he ist so good. He splits the kindling and chops the wood." Had Mother read that to me years ago? She must have. But when did she ever read to me? It would have had to be when I was very young, before my sisters left. But when? And were they there to listen, too? And where would Mother get the book? Did she go to the library? Even more than the words, I felt her voice, so warm as she read them, as though she was sharing a memory with me of someone she had known. Filling with tenderness, I tried to remember that moment, but it all remained blank—sudden tears stung my eyes.

After Marilyn and Ellin left, she arranged for me to take lessons, wanting the piano to be used. My favorite book became Stephen Foster's songs, and I played them over and over. If Mother was preparing supper while I practiced, I knew she was listening when she moved dishes and pans quietly instead of banging them. Once she said how pretty the piece was that I had played: "Beautiful Dreamer." I played it whenever she was in the kitchen. I found a book in the library: *He Heard America Sing, the Story of Stephen Foster,* and read it three times.

Growing stiff on my tree branch I slid down the rope, but lingered, sitting on the grass as I filled with another memory. My twelfth birthday. Why was I suddenly remembering that night? Aside from Mary Jo wishing me happy birthday earlier in the day, I didn't think anyone knew and, being shy, I didn't mention it. My Girl Scout troop was having a slumber party at our leader's house to celebrate our closure as a group. Those who wanted would go on to the older girls' Troop the next month. Night settled around us as we roasted our hot dogs and ate potato chips and pork-n' beans beside the fire. Our leader went into the house, then appeared carrying a large cake with twelve candles lighting her way. Mother appeared in the doorway behind her, watching. Everyone gathered around, singing to me, and cheered when I blew out the candles. I looked up at Mother. She smiled shyly at me. Our leader began cutting the cake, and—as though someone punched me, leaving me breathless—I saw what it was: a seven-layer chocolate cake. Mother had never baked one before.

One of my favorite books I discovered in the library when I was a little girl was *Little Brown Koko Has Fun*. It tells the adventures of a little colored boy with his small brown dog, and his "big, ole, good, fat, black Mammy." I loved this story of a little boy and his kind mother, a mother who was always there when he got into trouble, to bandage a bleeding knee, kiss a bumped head, or help him understand what had gone wrong to make him feel better. To show how much she loved him, regardless of what he had done, she would bake him a seven-layer chocolate cake with thick chocolate frosting. I renewed that book so often, Mother bought it for me. I still had the well-worn book on the shelf in my bedroom, but I hadn't thought about it for years. I looked at the huge cake, at the slices being served, and heard the ohs and ahs of the girls—they had never seen such a cake. Mother sat apart from our group and ate a small slice at our leader's insistence, but then disappeared.

Now, as I remembered that special night when I had become queen of the slumber party, I felt confused and teary-eyed.

Why had things always been so difficult between Mother and me? Why hadn't Mother joined the rest of us that night and shared it with me, eaten her cake with us? Why had she remained so distant the next day when I tried to thank her, when I tried to tell her how much fun it had been for everyone, when I tried to tell her what a special gift she had given me for my birthday?

I leaned against the trunk of the tree and tried to figure it out. She did these special things for me, but then wouldn't talk about them or acknowledge them, and before I knew it, caught off-guard, she'd hurl another angry accusation at me. Despite what I heard her tell the customer that day, she must still resent me. Her words I had grown up with still seared into my memory, how everything would have been better if only I hadn't been born.

✍ ✍ ✍

Two weeks later, with Daddy driving, the three of us left Marion and headed east. We were silent, a shy silence. We had never done anything like this before. We sat awkwardly staring out the windows. When we drove over a stretch of highway where the tar had swollen in the cracks between slabs of concrete, the car rhythmically bumping over them, Daddy dryly commented that the car had eaten too many onions. We burst into laughter, grateful for him breaking the silence. For miles whenever we hit a rough spot, one of us would call out "too many onions" and the others would laugh. It was Daddy who spied the first Burma Shave series of billboards and read them aloud as we passed. This became a contest as to who could see the next one first. That person got to read it aloud. I strained forward, peering from my back seat, and almost always was the first to call out. I knew they were letting me win, but even this felt good. We were learning how to have fun together.

When we arrived at the State Park in Bardstown, Kentucky, we toured the historic mansion that had inspired Stephen Foster to write "My Old Kentucky Home." The large house was filled with the magnificent paintings, sculptures, and luxurious furnishings of its prosperous plantation owner. We learned the Foster family themselves had lived in Pennsylvania yet supported the slavery that had made this plantation possible, though the guide quickly passed over this response to a question.

Stephen Foster, known as "the father of American music," captured the spirit of the South at that time in his songs, with all its beauty and prejudices: "Oh! Suzanna," "Sewanee River," "Old Black Joe," "Beautiful Dreamer," and his most famous, "My Old Kentucky Home."

Though I felt in awe of all the magnificence, I was disappointed to learn this wasn't where Stephen Foster lived or composed his music. That happened in the Foster family home in Pennsylvania. I had hoped to see his piano where he sat and first played the pieces I now played. Still, Stephen Foster had spent time here, and it inspired him to write his most famous song. He had walked where I now walked.

We stopped at a nearby restaurant for a late lunch. As Daddy and Mother read the menu, they looked at each other and—without a word, got up—and we left. Outside, Mother said a picnic would be much more fun, so we searched for a grocery store. We found a magnolia tree beside a back road and spread a blanket beneath it—the plush teal-colored auto-touring blanket Daddy's parents had given him as a college graduation present. Mother opened a loaf of Wonder Bread and a package of sliced American cheese. For dessert, she popped open a jar of home-canned peaches, to go with a bag of chocolate chip cookies. Daddy pried off the lids of bottled soft drinks: orange crush for me and root beers for both of them. I declared this was much better than eating in that restaurant. When Daddy belched loudly, Mother said that was the signal for us to start for Lexington.

Deep into Kentucky's horse country, Mother and Daddy stopped the car by the side of a dirt road to study the map. They had driven off the main road to see more of the farms, and now they were lost. I got out to lean against a nearby white fence and gaze across the emerald-colored field. A pleasant breeze brushed my face. Even though it was August, the air was sweet and everything looked green and fresh, a verdant blanket seeming to spread on forever. Young colts and fillies romped while their thoroughbred mothers grazed nearby. I imagined the best of these newborns one day would become a champion. I might be watching the next Man-o-War.

The day before, we had visited The Home of the Kentucky Derby. Before we joined our tour group to enter the sprawling, multi-storied white building, we strolled around the grounds. Mother and Daddy focused on what plants were selected to form the huge letters "Churchill Downs" at the entrance, and the other choices for the flowerbeds, each bed giving a different effect. A life-sized statue of a horse stood in the center of the largest flower bed. I studied it, and gawking upward, saw the Derby flags fluttering from green turrets on the buildings.

Inside, covered by that roof with the turrets, we sat in seats looking across the grounds. Red rose bushes tumbled around the owners' platform, which was across from the winner's circle, where they draped the horseshoe of roses over the champion's neck and presented the trophy to the owners. The entire complex was immense, the track seeming to stretch forever. I imagined what it must be like on race day, these seats filled with screaming people, the horses and their brightly attired jockeys restlessly lining up before thundering down the track, the roar of the crowd climaxing as the horses pounded toward the finish line. An electric tingle zipped throughout my body.

Back in the car, we found Calumet Farm, entered the white gates, and continued along a tree-lined drive to the man directing visitors to a lot nearest the information building. Daddy found a space at the end of a long line of parked cars. The farm, larger than I expected, bristled with activity. Multiple white barns surrounded fenced paddocks filled with trainers working with perfectly groomed horses. The air rang with the sounds of their voices and thudding hooves, and an occasional whinny. The family's residence, a rambling white house with a wrap-around porch, was positioned so they could look over the entirety of their vast farm. I stared at the second story and chose one of the bedroom windows for my own, drifting into a rich fantasy of what it would be like to live here.

In the car, Daddy had carefully counted some bills from their shoe box and now bought me a ticket to join a tour. He had looked at the dwindling money and said he and Mother preferred to sit in the chairs beneath the trees. I waited with a group of people, noticing I was the only young person.

Before we started, our guide told us the history of the farm, sharing information about the family and their proud lineage of champions. He emphasized the years of investment and commitment required to breed even one champion. This farm had produced many. He said we were privileged to visit the most prestigious horse farm in the world.

Our first stop was the cemetery for their champions. The guide unlocked the gate so we could wander among the graves. Each had a granite monument taller than I was, with a photo encased in the stone. It showed the horse in the Derby winner's circle, a garland of roses draped over the horse's neck, the owner accepting the silver cup. Life-sized bronze statues stood on several graves. I studied every photo, jumping to avoid swiveling sprinkler sprays moistening the grass. Although lush grass blanketed each of the memorials, I noticed there were no flowers.

In my pet cemetery at home, there were graves for Pal (the fluffy mongrel who followed me home, later hit by an alfalfa truck) Pepsi (my next dog, also hit by a truck), and Pansy (my calico stray, who birthed her litter of kittens in the middle of my bed). There were places for the baby robin (who fell from its nest), an unclaimed cat (who was smashed in the street, that I scooped into a shoe box, took home and buried), and the rabbit (found dead among the weeds). On each grave, I stuck a wooden marker on which I wrote the name in crayoned letters, then laid a sprig of flowers beside it. Mother always gave me something when I asked. During the cold months, she fixed artificial flowers, their vivid colors poking through the snow. In spite of the impressive monuments, this cemetery for Calumet's horse champions seemed sterile without flowers. I knew Mother would agree and reminded myself to tell her about this.

The guide led us past the training areas into one of the barns. We followed him along the wood-planked corridor, listening to him relate the heritage and records of each horse. Every stall had the horse's name and photo beside its door. Several were famous champions; all had been sired by Man-o-War.

The guide's voice faded as I gazed around. How could a barn be this clean? No odor of steaming dung, no acrid fly spray, not even dust motes floating in the beams of light—only the aroma of fresh sweet hay, mingled with that of horses, but an aroma I had never smelled before. Bathed and groomed daily, these horses smelled clean and earthy. I listened to the munching of oats, the muffled clump of a hoof on hay-covered floor, the soft chortling breaths.

We entered the hushed stillness of a smaller barn. I glanced upward. The ceiling was vaulted, like a cathedral, muted beams of sunlight shining down toward the center like soft spotlights. The only sounds were those of our footsteps following our guide. We stopped in front of a quadruple-sized stall. "Ladies and Gentlemen. Man-o-War."

His stall had no name or photograph. At our final stop, the farm's museum, there was an entire wall covered with his records, photographs, news clippings, ribbons and trophies. Man-o-War had sired over two hundred champions since his retirement from racing more than twenty years earlier. At this point in history, no other horse had ever equaled him.

Then, suddenly, there he stood, a trainer by his side holding his lead rope. Forcing my way to the front of the group, I stared up at him. I had never seen a horse like him. He was magnificent. Poised and motionless, he held his head high and stared straight ahead, not a muscle rippling. His ruby-chestnut coat, responsible for his nickname "Big Red," gleamed to a near glisten.

Amazement and love flooded through me, leaving me light-headed. I couldn't believe I was really here. Looking up at him I began pouring myself out silently to him—how I had dreamed and dreamed of meeting him, how I had studied his photographs and memorized everything about him in the magazines, how I had longed to watch him race at Churchill Downs and, as the grand champion, prance into the winner's circle where they draped the roses over his neck.

It happened in a fleeting moment, a moment that caught his trainer unaware, accustomed as he was to this superbly trained horse remaining still through countless viewings. The lead rope slipped through the trainer's hands as Man-o-War dipped his head and lowered his face to a level with my own, his luminous eyes peering into mine. I reached out and lay my hand on his muzzle. "Don't touch him!" shouted the trainer, pulling the horse's head up. I jumped and backed away, and said I was sorry—but I wasn't. Moist droplets clung to my skin where Man-o-War's lips had softly brushed my cheek.

Greatness caressed me that day at Calumet Farm, an experience that remains so clear in my memory. Yet in remembering that moment, I recall that other touch, linked also to my love of horses, when I learned that greatness isn't limited to world-famous champions. It can also be felt in the gentle touch of kindness, from a sheriff on a dusty field in Kansas.

The Pencil Collector

◡

In October, Daddy, his face flushed, rushed home from his coffee downtown with the news. To stimulate trade in our small town, the council decided to host a county-wide hobby show. It would be held in the basement of our city auditorium in two weeks, and on that Saturday night they would close off one block on Main Street for an October harvest square dance with live music. Daddy had signed up already for a booth to display his pencil collection. Would we help him get ready?

I couldn't remember ever seeing Daddy excited, but now—his face rosy, his eyes eager—my heart quickened. I wanted my parents to be happy, to recapture some of those lighter moments we had shared during our vacation. Since returning, we had settled into the old routine of all work and no smiles. Perhaps Mother felt the same way. Both she and I said we'd like to help him. Just tell us what to do.

When my parents ordered special cut flowers they couldn't grow in Kansas, like roses or gardenias, they arrived by train, packed in 3X4 foot special floral cardboard boxes. The cardboard had been heavily waxed inside to contain moisture. The flowers were stacked among layers of wet newspaper and ice. Daddy disappeared into the garage and returned with a stack of these box lids.

Laying one on the table, he studied it, then began making short pencil lines. He asked Mother for some elastic, the kind she used for sewing the waistbands on the skirts she made for me out of chicken-feed sacks. He measured the elastic against one of the lines and began cutting numerous pieces. He explained we would sew a strip on each line, securing it at each end. Hundreds of strips. Each loop would hold a pencil. As he held the lid up, we saw how the lines formed the shape of a tree. He grew more animated as he began sketching different designs on the other lids. "How do you know how to do this?" I asked him. His face brightened. "I saw these at a pencil convention once. You should see some of the things they create using only pencils. They even make free-standing structures like log cabins, sky scrapers, and the Golden Gate Bridge."

That night after the floral shop closed and we finished supper, Mother and I cleared the table while Daddy spread out the lids and materials, and the three of us began. For each strip of elastic, we had to poke our thick needles through the heavy wax of the cardboard plus through the elastic, tugging the stout corded thread back and forth through the layers twice, before knotting it on the back. We only had two thimbles, which we shared, each of us taking our turn using the back of a spoon instead of a needle to press the needle. This was hard as it kept slipping off the needle. Daddy used the spoon most of the time. He always took on the hardest part of any job, which usually made me feel sorry for him. He never complained, but I was grateful when he took the spoon from my hand and gave me his thimble. I was having trouble pressing my needle through even with a thimble.

For hours, night after night, we hunched over our work pushing and pulling our needles and thread. Neither Mother nor I grumbled, even when our thumbs ached and grew blistered and punctured. We had never done anything like this as a family, even during those fun moments this summer on our vacation. Huddled around the kitchen table, united in our project, an unfamiliar feeling of closeness developed between us that grew more palpable each time Daddy leaned another finished lid against the end of the piano. We would pause to stretch our hands, smiling. One more done.

Finally, on the night before the show, we finished. Daddy rose from the table with a secretive smile and disappeared into the garage. He returned with his arms loaded with shoe boxes—boxes filled with pencils. As he began opening them, I stared, speechless. Even Mother seemed surprised by how many he had.

He laid several lids on the floor, and for each design he sorted through his boxes for the right pencils. After he laid them out, Mother and I pushed each one into an elastic strip. He showed us how to make sure each pencil was straight, so the printing was legible, checking every pencil when we finished, pulling some out to position them better or at times replacing one for better effect. I watched as the strips of elastic transformed into magical designs. Clusters of richly hued sticks of wood began to take shapes. The first lid we did, the tree, was simple yet seemed wonderful to me. Various shades of brown pencils transformed into the trunk, shades of green became foliage. There were lids with various arrangements of flowers, others with multicolored geometric designs. Daddy made several lids simply of pencils from various countries, arranging them so people could read the languages printed on each pencil.

The lid that Daddy seemed most proud of, however, was his one displaying unique pencils that had been the hardest for him to collect, the rare ones. There were ones from World War II that did not come with erasures or ferrules (the brass bands). On the end was the phrase: "Rubber and Metal Gone to War." Another said: "Rubber Once Used for Eraser Now Used to Rub Out the Japs." The bullet pencils came from this same era. These looked like rifle cartridges. Daddy showed us how the "bullet" could be pulled out and attached the opposite way, transforming to full-length pencil, but when put back inside it became a five-inch cavity that kept a variety of interchangeable colored tips. There were several that Daddy called "lefties," which delighted him since he was left-handed. He showed us how the text could only be in the correct position to be read when it was held in the left hand, whereas a "righty" pencil's text would only be correct when held in the right hand. I moved from lid to lid, lightly tracing my fingers around their shapes. They seemed like miracles—worth my raw thumb.

We helped him load the lids into our delivery van, placing each lid carefully and spreading a bed sheet between each one. At the auditorium, I held the doors while Mother and Daddy carried the pallets of pencils to our booth. Daddy had secured a corner booth, which he said was lucky for it gave him two walls for display. We shuffled the lids around in different arrangements, Mother and I standing back to judge the effect, shifting the designs to their best advantage while Daddy made sure every pencil could be read.

While Daddy and Mother finished our booth, I wandered around to look at the other displays. Salt and pepper shakers were a popular hobby, and there were numerous booths displaying hundreds, each set different. Also, thimbles. I had no idea there were so many different shapes and colors. How I wished we had had one of the big sturdy ones during the last two weeks. Match-books were another popular collection. Several booths had rows of antique barbed wire—could there really have been this many different kinds? One booth had shelves holding hundreds of differ-ent praying hands, another had figures of the Madonna, each one different. Then came the ceramic collections of cats, dogs, horses and pigs. One booth had stacks and stacks of cowboy hats, each one a different shape or color, with an entire row of children's hats. Several women exhibited their handwork of crocheted pieces or patchwork quilts, intricate designs with thousands of stitches.

Daddy had the only pencil collection. The next morning when the show opened, I took up my station nearby where I could watch Daddy, my body rigid, asking God to please have people like his booth. He wore his suit, which Mother had pressed so the trouser creases stood crisp from his thighs to his ankles. His light blue tie and white shirt appeared radiant beside his ruddy face and balding head, crimson from months of working in the sun. For the next two days, Daddy stood waiting for someone to look at his pencils.

A few people paused at his booth to express surprise at the designs made out of pencils, but no one looked at Daddy. As they walked by, perhaps giving a quick glance his way, I saw the smile on Daddy's face turn wooden, his left ankle turning back and forth just as it had the time he stood once to give an announcement in church. The old fear crept into my heart. I needed him too strong to be wounded. When the rare person stopped to talk to him, I pretended everything was all right—until the next people passed by without looking. My eyes stinging, I wanted to run across to Daddy and hug him and tell him how much I loved his pencils.

On the final afternoon, I saw him point to a particular pencil for someone, drawing attention to something unusual, and the person looked closer and chuckled. Noticing this, several people stopped and clustered around. I listened to Daddy's voice as he explained the unique features, how his voice rose with an authority I had not heard before.

That night, when the show closed, the three of us dismantled Daddy's booth and loaded the lids back into the van. At home, Mother made hot cocoa with marshmallows and buttered toast with cinnamon sugar. We sat around the table, assuring Daddy how nice his booth had looked, and expressing our certainty his display had been the best in the show. No one else had anything so original. Sipping our cocoa, the three of us lapsed into a tired but comfortable silence, a different kind we never before had shared.

Daddy got up from the table and slowly began pulling the pencils out of their elastic holders and returning them to their boxes. He said he'd like to do this himself, to make sure they were put in the right boxes. I thought he simply wanted to linger a bit longer with his display by himself. When he got to his elaborate designs, he hesitated, reluctant to pull them apart. The lids crowded our small living area. He looked at them for long moments, then carried them to the garage, where he leaned them against the shovels and rakes hanging from the wall. But the car might bump them, so he moved them up to the storage loft. Months later when I climbed up to get something, I found them in a corner, covered with dust.

For a few days, customers commented politely on Daddy's collection. I watched his face light up as he talked about his pencils. But he soon realized they weren't really interested, and soon no one mentioned his collection again. Daddy's silence lengthened into longer and longer periods, filled with melancholy. It seemed the last of something important simply drained out of him.

Though we never talked about it, I remembered those nights we came together as a real family for the first time, working to prepare the pencils, celebrating with marshmallow cocoa and cinnamon toast. For one brief moment we shared something special, glimpsing what might have been, before drifting apart again.

Moving On

〰

When I left home, I never asked my parents for a penny—I knew they didn't have one to give. Working two part-time jobs to get started, I scratched my way through college and graduate school, earning my ticket to escape from the life into which I had been born: a degree in clinical psychiatric social work.

To my surprise, when I ranked first and led our Master's class in the procession of graduates into Washington University's stadium in St. Louis, it was Mother who drove the distance to watch and snap photos. That evening, she sat gracious and beaming through our class celebration banquet, exuding the glow of belonging. I had never seen her like this before. She had had her hair done, put on makeup, and wore her best dress. We were a mother and daughter enjoying an important experience together, a first for us both. I felt so proud of her, though shadowed with sadness for all that we had missed, the relationship we might have had.

At times, I wonder. Even though she disparaged me as a Newsom—Daddy's girl who embodied his traits she scorned—wasn't I the daughter who carried her traits even more, those qualities that enabled her to survive? Didn't I carry her fierce determination, both of us refusing to let anything defeat us? Her circumstances from the beginning combined to trap her, but through me some of her dreams did come true. She had hungered for an education but was denied that opportunity. I was her only daughter who attended and finished college. As I observed her happiness at our class banquet, I realized she was sharing the joy of what I had achieved. I felt more pleased for her than for myself, so grateful I had been able to give this to her.

❧ ❧ ❧

My first job was joining the staff of an acute care psychiatric hospital in Kansas City, Missouri. From the head of our department, a devout Roman Catholic, I learned about a man who had intended to become a Roman Catholic priest, but, when an increasing number of homeless or abused adolescent boys came to him for help, he believed his calling had changed. He bought a large run-down farmhouse on the outskirts of the city to provide a home for these boys and scrounged whatever resources he could find for support. Over the years, it would grow to become a thriving home and would include a residential treatment center and school, but in the beginning, it was a struggle. I secured a part-time job there on weekends, donating many extra hours.

One Saturday morning, when I arrived at the home, I walked by two very muddy men digging a ditch across the front yard. One leaned on his shovel, grinned at me, and explained the water line had broken. There were no funds for repair. He introduced himself as Roy, the new volunteer president of the newly formed board of directors for the boys' home, and his friend, George, a local physician and personal friend, whom Roy had persuaded to provide free medical care for the boys as well as join him on the board. The home was in crisis that morning: "Try having twenty-six teenage boys wake up to no water," Roy said.

With a mocking laugh, George quipped: "Just what I expected to be doing as the doctor and board member, but what the hell, what else would I have to do on a Saturday morning?" He jabbed his shovel back into the muck.

Several days later, Roy called and asked if we could go for dinner. He wanted me to explain the treatment program the home was establishing for the boys. He was a pleasant man in his middle thirties, a stocky build, his face not handsome, yet strong, with its Germanic-heritage features and prematurely gray hair receding at his temples. I noted a social clumsiness, an innocence, which, for whatever reasons, I found endearing. It took several more meals at Pancake Shack (all he could afford, I discovered) to realize his intentions were not solely to learn about the program.

Roy had suffered severe learning disabilities as a youngster, and, failing in the regular school system, transferred to a trade school for his high school years. No one in his extended family had any formal education (they had worked traditional blue-collar jobs), but Roy was determined to rise above this.

A few months after we met, on a balmy summer evening, Roy and I sat on the grass beside the art gallery's cascading fountain, eating ice cream cones. I listened as he shared his dream: to invent a product of his own—not to get rich (for if he did things right he felt certain he would be comfortable), but to have that feeling of creating something that would be the best in the world. To ensure the quality, he would have to manufacture and distribute the product himself. He had the image of a three-legged milk stool, each leg having to be balanced for everything to function well: excellent product; excellent customer service; and delivery on time. He had been searching for an idea he could develop.

After the Navy, he had worked on an assembly line in a manufacturing plant while he saved his money, taking on odd jobs to do on a used lathe machine he bought and set up in his garage. Since before the Navy in his late teens, he had been supporting his family: a homebound father who slowly died of cancer, a young brother, and a totally dependent mother.

His break finally came when he learned of the frustrating absence of an accurate pressure switch regulating oil tanks in the field, resulting in inaccuracies and wasteful spillage. Roy began developing a switch that would be dead-accurate. At the time we met, he had moved out of his garage into a small building in the industrial section, and was assembling a few switches. These he loaded into his station wagon and traveled around the country, trying to place them in the field free of charge, desperate for people to try them.

Although my friends and parents liked Roy immediately, a congenial "salt-of-the-earth" guy, they were surprised when we married, expecting me to choose an educated, professional man. Why had I said yes? Did I recognize in him a kindred spirit? Over pancakes and ice cream cones, I had become acquainted with a man who had had a harsh boyhood with almost every strike against him, but through sheer will was determined to rise above it. As I listened to him, I knew one day he would achieve his dream, a dream I knew I could support. I realized he was a strong family man, as well as someone I could take home to meet my family without embarrassment or shame, certain he would accept them and not judge them, or me.

Yet, I made my decision before I received help to understand myself and work through my demons, and in spite of all my efforts, I ended up choosing my husband in ways not unlike my parents. Like my father's missionary idealism led him to Mother's aid, my caseworker training and compassion filled me with a desire to help this man who had no one; like my mother, though concerned about my absence of passion, I felt safe with Roy and settled for a good man who really wanted me. Although I fared better than my parents, whose relationship was burdened from the start with complications, I soon realized my mistake—I had not been ready to choose a life partner. Yet Roy and I established a marriage that was positive in many ways for both of us. He gave everything to it that he had to give, and I in turn was a strong support for him over the years as his dream came true. He developed into the confident leader of his own company, a company that produced a pressure switch that was recognized worldwide as the best in industry.

At our wedding on a beautiful day in May, two of the boys from the boys' home where we met served as our ushers.

⌁ ⌁ ⌁

From the very beginning, Roy felt right at home with my family, including Mother's strong, eccentric ways. He chuckled whenever he recalled their first meeting, that day we drove to my parents' home in Marion. We pulled into their driveway to find Mother in bib overalls on the garage roof repairing shingles. She called down a few unintelligible words through nails clamped in her mouth, pounded in several more, then scooted down the roof to the ladder. He noticed her wisps of gray hair sticking in all directions from under the multi-colored cap she'd knit from leftover bits of yarn, and her faded patchwork jacket with several buttons missing, fastened together with oversized safety pins. She took the nails out of her mouth and demanded why he hadn't climbed up to help her? When he shot back that she hadn't asked him, I saw the surprised, playful glint in her eyes.

While I observed them as they bantered on, I was seeing the Mother who emerged during our visit to her dad's floral complex in Illinois all those years ago, where she talked and joked comfortably with the hired men she had worked with as a kid. Apparently, Roy felt the same homey comfort with her. Through the years, whenever she became difficult, he could say "Oh come on now, Gertrude," and she'd laugh at herself and the incident would be over. Years later, when he spoke at her funeral, he challenged whether any man present had given his mother-in-law as successful a Mother's Day gift as he had one year: a vise for her workbench.

Final Journeys

❧

After a third devastating flood, years after I had left home, my parents abandoned their valley property and rebuilt on the hill near the city limits. To my surprise, Mother's dad financed them. The flood had wiped them out and they had to rebuild from scratch. In spite of all his gruffness, once again when Mother really needed him, he had come through. He dealt only with her, though, still avoiding my father.

Life became somewhat easier for them, and years later they sold their greenhouse and retired. With this transition, their relationship also shifted. Perhaps they no longer buried themselves in business chores as a way to avoid each other. Perhaps they needed each other in new ways as they aged. Perhaps they just let go of a lifetime of regrets and accepted their situation. Whatever the reasons, they developed a tender compatibility, and made peace with their lonely life together.

On the evening of February 13, 1979, a week before his seventy-third birthday, Daddy called for Mother to help him from the bathroom after suffering a sudden weakness. As they lurched toward the bedroom, Daddy said: "Oh, gosh, tomorrow's Valentine's Day and I don't even have a Valentine for you."

"That's all right, Pop," Mother said. "We'll make cookies together." But Daddy collapsed and died from heart failure before they reached their bed.

The bitterly cold day of his funeral, the church echoed with emptiness. Three women from the church were there out of respect for Mother, and Lorraine plus two of my high school classmates attended to support me. Daddy's obituary mentioned his familiar "What's new?" greeting, by which he had become known, these simple words that seemed humorous to townspeople but couldn't begin to reveal his yearning all those years to be let into someone's life.

ꙮ ꙮ ꙮ

Two days after Mother phoned to tell me Daddy had died, I was at my parents' house alone, having gone to Marion to help her prepare for his funeral. There was a knock at the back door. Local people would come to the front door to pay their respects, although no one came. I tensed. Before Mother left on errands, she told me the Denver people were on their way. Denver people? Could this be Marilyn, coming for the services? Had Mother known where to find her to let her know? I hadn't seen her for almost thirty years. She faded completely from my life after she moved with her two babies and left no forwarding address. I turned the knob, my hand shaking.

Ellin stood there alone. She burst into tears. "Can you ever forgive us?" She stood wringing her hands, remorse twisting her tear-stained face.

I pulled her into the room, held her shoulders and looked into her eyes. "For what?"

"For what we did to you that night. You were so little, and so scared." Fresh tears bathed her cheeks.

I knew what she was talking about. Although I suffered other damaging trauma as a child, that night with the knife at my throat was the worst. Even after years of therapy, some little thing would happen that triggered the experience all over again. Yet I meant it when I gathered her into my arms. "There's nothing to forgive, Ellin—we were all just kids, trying to survive."

She pulled away and burst into fresh tears. "No one has ever forgiven me before. I don't deserve it. I know we hurt you. I'm so sorry." Wracking sobs. Eventually her crying slowed. "You really forgive me? All these years. This is a miracle. I wish Marilyn could be here to feel your forgiveness, too." She hadn't known where to reach Marilyn to tell her of Daddy's death, but she felt certain she wouldn't have come anyway. Ellin said that since Marilyn became a born-again Christian, she had agonized over what she had done to me that night, remaining too ashamed to face me. That was the reason she disappeared out of my life.

I tried to absorb what Ellin was saying. During my brief meeting in Denver with Marilyn years ago, I had realized she was terribly distraught, that her difficult life continued to be filled with suffering. I left Denver wondering whether she still resented and blamed me for most of it. I didn't know. Through the years, whenever there had been an unexpected knock at my door, that old fear often gripped me. If I opened the door, would I discover Marilyn poised to plunge the blade, wanting revenge for all her suffering? This threat I had lived with since I was five years old still was often triggered. But did I understand Ellin correctly, that Marilyn no longer felt rage toward me, that instead, her suffering had included anguish, guilt and shame for what she had done to me?

Heartache clenched my chest. Our family had lived with so much pain during those early years, trauma that had damaged each one of us. And no one ever talked about any of it. Daddy died shut down with depression, trapped and defeated by life. Mother merely existed, isolated in her own little world. Marilyn and Ellin lived shattered lives. As soon as I finished my education and had an income, I sought help. Following years of therapy, I had found a degree of healing and peace. None of my family had had that privilege. Could I now help my sisters? But it wouldn't happen. They had their own stories, and their damage scarred too deep. Even after this moment together, Ellin shied away from even a superficial relationship with me, and I would never find Marilyn.

It would be decades before I finally understood that I never had been responsible for any of my sisters' suffering, and it wasn't my responsibility or capability to try to fix them.

◦ ◦ ◦

I continue to subscribe to the Marion newspaper, and recently found a tidbit in the remembrance section for December 1950:

"It probably won't happen again in many years, but five bald-headed gentlemen are pictured sitting down in a row to have their morning coffee. It happened Friday at Coon's Restaurant. The counter line-up for the now organized "Bald-Headed Coffee Club" includes: (five names were listed, including the dentist, a gas station operator, my father the florist, the welfare director, and a car dealer.)"

By virtue of his bald head, after many years, my father had found a niche with those men, just by dropping into the cafe every morning. Beside their baldness, the only other thing they shared was their pleasure having a morning cup of coffee in the camaraderie of a café.

Over time, Daddy had been accepted good-naturedly by our small town as one of their characters, though he was mostly ignored. He never had a friend, and never did anything socially other than meet for a cup of coffee with these men for several years. His photo appeared in the paper again, in recognition for the amount of blood he donated at the Red Cross blood drives through the years: twelve gallons at that time. He also received recognition for volunteering to assume leadership of the Girl Scouts organization, but I don't know how that turned out.

Eventually his greatest pleasure came through his hobby collecting pencils. He joined the Kansas State Pencil Collector's Club and, until his health began to fail, never missed their meetings held periodically in the larger cities throughout the state. For years he found recognition and companionship out of town with these fellow collectors. Only after he died did I discover, through a phone conversation with the President of the Kansas Pencil Collectors' Club, that, although the records going back that far weren't complete, Daddy was thought to have been one of their founding members and was held in esteem. The President told me he had envied my dad's collection, which had ranked as one of the best in the country.

～ ～ ～

Soon after Daddy's funeral, without telling Roy or me, Mother sold her house. We hurried to Marion as soon as her pastor phoned me her circumstances. She had retained the back half of the property, had not yet vacated the house, and we found her in back digging a hole. She was constructing an earth house for herself, convinced it would serve her nicely. Having dug down about three feet, all she needed to do was dig several more feet down and make it wider, then stretch a tarp over the top, and she'd be fine. Looking at me scornfully, she added she didn't need to be fancy like me. I turned it over to Roy. He convinced her to let us buy her a house trailer. When it was in place on a poured concrete basement, we arranged for the construction of an attached garage and a small greenhouse. For the next thirteen years, Mother lived content, planted organic gardens and fruit trees, and puttered in her basement ceramics studio Roy and she built together.

When I helped Mother move into her trailer home, I lied to her for the first and only time I could remember. As we settled her new kitchen, she fretted. "Where is my favorite knife?" I assured her it was probably still packed in one of the boxes and would show up. After everything was unpacked and she still couldn't find it, feigning bewilderment I took her to buy a new one, but that one never pleased her, and she continued to grumble about her loss. I never confessed, and never felt one shred of guilt. I had buried that old butcher knife deep in the trash barrel.

⌒⌒⌒

The autumn after we moved Mother into her new home, Roy and I enrolled our two young children, a son and a daughter, in a private school near our home. I requested a meeting with the nutritionist who supervised the dining room. The students gathered daily for family-style meals. Both of our children suffered food allergies, but if our son ate the wrong thing, it would result in a trip to the hospital emergency room. I expected to send sack lunches. I liked Fern Pine, the nutritionist, immediately. As we chatted comfortably, suddenly she stopped and exclaimed: "You're Rendel Newsom's daughter! Oh, my goodness. I was his classmate through high school and college in Emporia, Kansas."

Speechless, I thought this couldn't be happening. It seemed unbelievable that—in this new life I had worked so hard to establish one hundred fifty miles from my hometown—I would have to deal all over again with my father's embarrassing reputation. I didn't want this to tarnish my children's experience at their new school. Would I need to find another place for them?

Yet as I listened, I heard Mrs. Pine describe what a wonderful young man my father had been—an honor student who was admired for his conscientiousness and high ideals, the most popular boy in school. She must be confusing him with someone else, or just being polite? This couldn't be my father she was talking about. I stared at her. She asked, "Did he reach his dream of teaching in an Indian school? I hope so—he was so good with children." My father?

Her eyes dreamy, she recalled their junior and senior class musicals, how the community attended enthusiastically because Daddy, with his superb bass voice, had the main roles. "His voice was professional, like his Mother's—but then you know that." But did I know he had been a paid soloist at two different churches every Sunday? "He worked Saturdays at a floral greenhouse, then Sundays singing—he had to help his family financially, you know, when his younger brother got so sick." Chuckling, she continued. "He would sing at one church, duck out the back door of the choir loft and race his bicycle several miles across town to the other church, climb in a back window and slip into their choir just in time for his second solo." She laughed heartily, then sobered. "He was so much fun—so playful! He always made everyone feel good. We called him the boy with the dancing eyes."

She paused, returning to the present. "Well, no one has ever brought sack lunches to my dining room, and I certainly can't let Rendel Newsom's grandchildren be the first. Give me a list of their allergies. I'll take good care of your children."

Later, I sat in my car in the parking lot, thinking of what she had told me. How could this be true? She spoke with such genuine warmth and admiration for my father. But how could anyone go from being the person she described to the man I experienced? What had so tragically changed him? I began to weep, overcome with sadness and compassion for my father—for the isolated, lonely and depressed man he had become, for the death of all he had been.

With astonishment, as I brooded on this, I flooded with love for him, the love that for most of my life I had not allowed myself to feel. In the beginning, I had been his special little girl, and I reveled in this, trusting he would protect me. But that night when he and Mother went to a movie, when my sisters tortured me with the knife, I realized he couldn't protect me. Worse, I realized that my being special to him increased my sisters' and Mother's resentment, and thus my danger. Caught in an impossible situation, not safe with anyone, I did the only thing a five-year-old little girl could do: I denied my love for him, buried it deep, and kept my distance.

As he had grown older and his behavior deteriorated, I interpreted this as his awkward attempts still to be socially accepted, trying to be funny, and I felt increasingly scornful. I recalled the time he and I went to the hardware store, how he began to talk to the clerk, but, instead of words, he babbled strange animal noises. Daddy had seemed surprised, but when the clerk laughed, with a pleased grin Daddy tried to repeat his nonsensical noises, seeming to have found a way to get this unexpected attention. I flushed with embarrassment. Since he repeated it, I assumed he could control it. And he frequently farted loudly, seemingly unconcerned. He had never fit into the social life of Marion, but this behavior made me angry. Couldn't he realize how inappropriate he was, how he brought his isolation on himself? I saw it for the first time when he took me with him to the cafe for morning coffee when I was little. That memory still stung. His behavior had only gotten worse through the years.

I had wanted the respect and acceptance of our community, and I separated from my family to get it, desperate to prove I was different from them. Only in retrospect, after his death, did I begin to suspect he might have been suffering with some slow developing neurological problem, and regretted not having asked for an autopsy. At that point, it couldn't have made any difference, but it might have shed light on some of my haunting questions.

I sat in my car, overwhelmed with my truth that I had buried all these years—the truth that I had been special to him even as he had been special to me. His gentle and loving presence during my earliest years, that man I experienced when we were companions alone in the greenhouse, had been the man Fern Pine described.

There are so many things I wish I could talk with him about, questions I want to ask him, do so many things differently. I never told him how much I loved him, never thanked him, never told him goodbye. I now realized I had never even known my father—all his accomplishments before he married, what he enjoyed doing, his boyhood dreams and aspirations. I had never heard him sing one note. And I never, ever, saw his eyes dance.

Even though so much about my father will always remain a mystery, one thing I do know is that, in spite of his best intentions, he became trapped in a marriage that was totally barren of love. From the very beginning, my parents lived together like strangers, completely wrong for each other. Both of them accepted their mistake, became stoical and silent, and buried themselves in their never-ending work. At times, just as she did with me, Mother seemed to get pleasure in ridiculing Daddy in front of others. I overheard her tell some customers how he joined the men's softball team when they first moved to Marion. She went to only one game and sat on an adjoining empty bleacher, apart from the other wives, reading her *Reader's Digest*. "I saw no reason to watch the game.

The only time I looked up, I saw the ball go right through his legs." She smirked, unaware of the implications for both of them of what she was saying, pleased when the customers laughed, not noticing their discomfort. Working nearby in the greenhouse, Daddy pretended he hadn't heard, but lowered his head, his face reddening.

Many people endure loveless relationships, but my parents—our entire family—lived with an element that went far beyond that, something I try hard to understand. I saw my mother become so different when she visited her friends in Illinois and later with my husband. But in Marion, with our family, she retreated into an impervious, cold armor, in which she became emotionally locked away. I never heard her say she loved any one of us, never received or saw her give anyone a hug or even a warm touch or an affectionate glance. She rebuffed my father's every attempt to express affection. All of us lived with an abandonment and loneliness, the depths of which are impossible to describe. Her verbal attacks against my father and me were cruel. What triggered these? Where did they come from? When she finally softened and tried to reach out to me during my late adolescence, the damage had been too deep for too long, and I couldn't respond in kind. She also was so unpredictable, I never felt safe with her. In their final years together, even though she and Daddy settled into a compatibility, it signified their resignation. They had missed having any kind of warm, caring relationship all of their lives together.

I can understand Daddy's descent into depression, but I struggle to comprehend his outbursts of violence that escalated into murderous rage. As I try to understand his behavior, I'm left with a combination of several complex issues, issues impossible for me to untangle and digest. How much did Mother's cold rejection followed by his frustration, loneliness and depression, trigger his explosions? His awareness he had turned his back on his rich potential and made an impulsive and tragic choice that trapped him in this marriage, this place he hated? If he did have a neurological deterioration, did that contribute to such uncontrollable outbursts? It's puzzling, for these outbursts stopped after my sisters left home. And he did control his fury earlier—the one time he began beating me but stopped. His love for me had proven stronger than his rage. Couldn't he have controlled his rage with my sisters?

After meeting with Fern Pine, through inquiries in Marion, I learned Daddy had had two car accidents during the year before his death, drifting into a ditch both times. Thank goodness he hadn't killed someone, they said. People thought he was a drunkard and they reacted with disgust.

After one of the accidents, he had stitches in his head, and the local doctor told him to lay off the booze. When I asked her, Mother said Daddy had just blacked out. We both knew he never touched alcohol. Did no one, including the doctor, think to consider a possible medical condition that should be looked into? But I wonder if the doctor (who is long deceased) understood more than he had communicated, or that he tried, and Mother couldn't hear or didn't understand? Long afterwards, she mentioned that, after the second accident, the doctor had told her Daddy would be incontinent, and she told him it wouldn't make any difference. She thought the word meant impotent.

I remembered the time Daddy called me just to say hello. During our conversation, I heard strange gurgles, then silence. Had he died? Did he need help? Mother must have been outside. I raced to another phone and called their neighbor. A short time later, the neighbor called to tell me that Daddy had just fainted and now was fine, sitting there smiling and feeling sheepish. It was a hot day; she and Mother thought he had overdone it in the garden.

I fear this tangled web that I keep trying to understand will remain elusive to me always, but I have to live with the awareness that Daddy had needed help, and I wasn't there for him. No one had been.

~ ~ ~

Thirteen years after Daddy died, at age eighty-six, Mother suffered a TIA (transient ischemic attack), a forewarning of a potential stroke. Although her body began to recover quickly, she had lost her sense of independence, and feared living alone one hundred fifty miles from us. With never a look back, she accepted our offer to move her to an assisted living apartment complex near us in Kansas City while she continued her recovery. I anticipated this to be an interim plan, that she would return to her home in Marion. But she continued to cling to us. I hoped this was a temporary reaction.

Promptly at 8:00 a.m. every day, I picked her up at her apartment and brought her to our home to putter in the ceramic studio she and Roy built for her in our basement. I prepared her lunch, took her drinks and snacks, and kept her company off-and-on during the day, then returned her at 5:00 p.m. for dinner in her residence dining room. I also took her to her numerous medical and rehabilitation appointments. Regardless of all that I did, however, nothing changed between us. I had turned into her handmaiden, but I remained the resented outsider.

Although I had taken on this role willingly, knowing Roy and I were the only ones Mother had to help her, I hadn't realized the toll it would take on my personal life. For some time, I remained steeped in denial. After the day she tried to make herself lunch at our home at 10:00 a.m., and I returned home to find an empty pan scorching on a burner turned to high, I realized I couldn't leave her alone even for a brief time. This meant I was no longer free to have a few hours for myself, which resulted in my painful decision to take a leave of absence from a local university program. I was two years into earning a degree in literature and the classics, completing the requirements necessary to apply to their graduate writing program, hoping at last to fulfill my long-deferred dream of a master's degree in creative writing.

Over the long lean years of our marriage, I had supported Roy as he slowly established his manufacturing plant. Our son's rehabilitation programs through the years had proven successful, correcting some problems he struggled with since birth, and both of our children had graduated from college. At last it had been my turn. I listened to my heart, and I returned to school to take classes that I had chosen for the right reasons. I loved my university program, ranked first in my class, and I had less than a year to go before entering the graduate writing program. Resentment at having to defer my plan began to gnaw at my spirit.

One complicated morning, I arrived fifteen minutes late to get Mother. She was striding back and forth by the receptionist's desk, stomping her cane with each step. When I rushed in, she said harshly, "It's about time." Then she turned to the receptionist and snapped, "She has always been a disappointment. I've never been able to count on her. I tried to sell her when she was born but no one would even give me a nickel for her."

Taken aback, the young woman looked at me. I was the only person in the entire complex who arrived every morning seven days a week to pick someone up. Hiding my quick tears of frustration, I fled to the car, passing rows of residents positioning their wheelchairs so they could people-watch until lunch.

When Mother climbed into the car, I turned on her. "I have heard you telling people that all my life. Do you have any idea how much it hurts?"

"Oh, you're so sensitive," she said coldly, staring straight ahead. "Well, let's go. I have a lot to do today."

Once again, I felt that iron door clang shut, making it useless for me to continue trying to talk with her. After moments of taking deep breaths, I turned the key.

The few times I have shared this part of my story in my writing groups, someone has always challenged me: why would I continue doing this? Why would I ever take care of my mother when she never took care of me? A question I had to answer for myself.

As a baby that first night home from the hospital, I lived because I came into this world with a spirit determined to survive. As a very young child, that same spirit led me into our neighborhood, knocking on doors, searching for the love that was absent in our home. I fill with gratitude whenever I recall those generous-hearted mother figures who opened their doors to me and nurtured me through those early years. Because of their caring, I have the capacity to make choices, which my mother never had. Faced with the challenge of assuming her care, how could I resort to an eye-for-an-eye response, abandoning that more loving path I had experienced and chosen for myself? Perhaps my choice was more for me than for her, I'm not sure. I believe it was for both of us. But I knew in my heart that, in spite of everything, it was the only choice I could make. I wouldn't abandon my mother, regardless of how difficult it became.

Some days Roy would take over and give me time for myself. He enjoyed being with Mother, helping her develop creative ideas in her workshop. Always brilliant in solving any kind of mechanical problem, he dealt with it as his playtime to support Mother's inventive spirit. He enjoyed their jaunts to the hardware stores to look for parts to build their ideas, or to the ceramic warehouses to search for a particular shade of paint. Secure and content, Mother seemed happier than I had ever seen her. I knew the best thing I had ever done for her was marrying Roy. She settled right into her new life with us, and after a few months asked us to sell her place in Marion.

Less than four years after her TIA, her hip broke. Everything changed. After her surgery and hospital recovery, I moved her to a nursing home that offered a good rehabilitation program. The surgeon warned me that—when he saw bones as spongy as hers—there was little expectation she would live more than a year. Still, familiar with Mother's determined spirit, I hoped she could heal and return to this life she now loved, and perhaps I could still return to the university. But her bones continued to crumble from advanced osteoporosis. Her other hip broke three months later. Another surgery. This time she had difficulty with the anesthetic and her recovery was slower. In less than a month the pins holding her soft bones in the first surgery slipped, and that leg twisted. The surgeon advised it would be a high risk to perform a third major surgery in less than five months, because she probably would not survive, yet if we didn't do it now it would be too late to correct the problem. I followed his advice not to risk having the surgery and had to explain to Mother she would never walk again. She would live her remaining life in this nursing home. Thus, her final journey began, a journey we both would share. But the surgeon was wrong about one thing. She lived for another three years.

When I took Mother to be admitted to the long-term care wing, Roy bowed out, apologizing, but he felt too uncomfortable around nursing homes. He had done his part. For Mother's remaining years, I was on my own.

Mysteries Revealed

R oy and I cared for Mother for seven years after we moved her to Kansas City following her TIA. Even with Roy's help, the first four of those years had been hard for me, as both Mother and I plunged back into the patterns of our turbulent relationship of my childhood. But after her hip broke, something slowly began to shift.

From the moment she learned she would never walk again, would never leave that nursing home, would never be able to get out of bed alone, Mother fell into several months of deep depression. Day by day, I watched her fierce independence and cold stoicism slowly crumble along with her bones as her body deteriorated. Slowly, over time, her rock-hard emotional armor dissolved, and the depth of her pain and sadness that the armor had hidden all those years began to emerge. A different Mother slowly became visible and more accessible. A new and surprising bond between us began to take shape and grow, the bond that would support our traveling through the journey of the next three years.

Whenever the weather permitted, I pushed her wheelchair into the garden, following the winding path, stopping so she could lean over to smell the flowers. Eventually we rested beside the goldfish pond and small waterfall in the center of the garden, spying a hopping frog or a darting fish, lulled by the splashing waters. During these hours, and while I sat beside her in her room, I began to ask questions, and she responded, sometimes more than others, sometimes not at all, but over a long period of time it allowed me to piece her story together.

I had often wondered, I first asked, how she and Daddy met and decided to marry? Neither of them had ever talked about it. It all began one summer at Grampa's floral complex, she said, soon after she left Henry. (Did I know about Henry, Marilyn and Ellin's father?) She had been working in her dad's office for several years, arranging for Ellin and Marilyn to stay with babysitters. Even though her father had banished her when she married Henry, when her circumstances became desperate, he had relented and let her return.

During the summers, Grandpa would hire several college boys to help out, and Daddy was one of the two that summer. He had finished college in May, an honor student with a double major, prepared to achieve his dream—teach in one of the reservation schools for American Indian children. The Presbyterian Church Board of Missions narrowed their decision down to two applicants, one of whom was Daddy. He hoped he would soon receive word of his acceptance. Meanwhile, he needed a job. He had worked weekends and summers through high school and college at a greenhouse in Emporia, Kansas. When his parents moved to Illinois to accept a pastorate there, he contacted the leading floral complex in the area (a complex owned by Grandpa) for a job and Grandpa hired him.

"Were you and Daddy interested in each other from the beginning?" I asked.

Mother snorted a harsh laugh, watching two koi fish swim across the pond before answering. For one of the upcoming dances, given monthly by her dad for his employees, she and the other office girl had drawn straws for the two summer workers. "I lost," Mother said. "I got Rendel. Even though I wasn't the least bit interested in him, he was someone to do things with. The four of us began double dating."

Several things happened during that summer. Grandpa ate his noon meal every day in the boarding house with his men. He sat at the head of the table and took this time to outline their schedule for the afternoon, but he sometimes bragged about his clever yet shady and barely legal moves that were resulting in his prosperous growth. Daddy was the only one who spoke up and challenged him, and one day, when Daddy went too far, in a rage Grandpa fired him. Mother ate lunch at the boarding house along with the men and witnessed this. She chuckled as she recalled the scene. The very next day Daddy received word that the other applicant had been chosen for the position at the Indian mission. It was the early 1930s, the whole country struggling through the depression, and Daddy needed to decide quickly what to do with his life.

Mother felt stagnated in her job and dependent on her father, but she had little money and nowhere to go. She yearned for a family for her two little girls. After Daddy was fired, realizing he would be leaving, she looked at him more seriously. "Even though I didn't love him, felt no physical attraction, I knew he was a good man." She overlooked what she considered his stuffy ways. I could imagine Daddy overlooked Mother's crude ways and lack of affection, and saw only that she and her two girls needed help. His missionary zeal must have risen to the front. The one and only thing they shared was knowledge of the floral business. They decided to pool their resources, get married, and buy the greenhouse they learned was for sale in Kansas, sight unseen.

Grandpa declared that, if Mother married this man, Grandpa would have nothing more to do with her, this time forever. Daddy's parents also were shocked at their son's choice of bride: divorced with two children, no education or respectable family. He and his wife would never be welcome in Daddy's parents' home either. Yet, the strange part was that his father, a Presbyterian minister, officiated at their wedding.

Daddy's father had been a Presbyterian minister and college professor of theology and philosophy, listed in America's Who's Who of distinguished scholars. He and his wife raised their five children with high ideals and a reverence for education. (For years, every Christmas I received a card from those grandparents that listed most of their grandchildren with their PhDs or number of years left before he or she would get one.) Their eldest son, also a distinguished scholar, would become Chancellor of New York University and, upon retirement there, became Senior Editor for Prentice-Hall Publishing Company. Another son became the Mayor of Whittier, California, active in politics and admired in that community. The third son became a high-level engineer with Boeing Industries. Daddy had prepared academically to take his respected place in their family. He lived by the ethics of his family. He never touched a cigarette or sipped a beer, and I never heard him utter a swear word. He didn't make an issue of this and never berated anyone else for these things, just quietly lived by his own standards. But to his parents and siblings, when he married Mother, moved to small-town Kansas, and became owner of a broken-down greenhouse, he had turned his back on all they stood for. He became their failure and he felt their scorn.

I wondered what my parents thought when they drove into the driveway that Fourth of July and viewed the disaster they had purchased in Marion. They had made a bargain together that trapped them unawares, two people as foreign to each other as they were to this new place where they were forced to settle. I never heard either of them complain. They shouldered their obligations and buried their feelings in stoic silence.

Yet, in the nursing home, when Mother told me this history, I understood another aspect of my parents' silence through the years. They were as different as night and day and, aside from the business, they didn't share one thing in common to talk about.

I continued going to the nursing home every day, arriving early and staying late, helping Mother with her limited rehabilitation activities, assisting her with meals, and in general making sure she received the care she needed. It was a good facility, but the staff couldn't give this kind of individual care to each person. She had become dependent on my being there, and fearful if I wasn't. The few times I missed a day, Mother resisted getting out of bed and often refused to eat.

During my college years, Ellin and I had begun exchanging Christmas and birthday cards, plus an occasional letter. I'm not clear how or why it began, but that meagre correspondence became her only link to her past. She and Mother seldom spoke and, like the rest of us, she had no contact with Marilyn. Over time, none of us knew how to even find Marilyn. I asked Ellin to come and give me a few day's help with caring for Mother, but she refused. Mother had become solely my responsibility.

Mother and I continued our conversations during her quiet hours. One day, I said I knew nothing about her as a little girl, and this prompted her telling me about her childhood. What unfolded was a heart-wrenching tale of a harsh and lonely life, that she shared with me without a shred of self-pity.

Her story had to begin with that of her mother, Mabel. Mabel had grown up on the palace grounds of the King of Sweden. Mabel was born in one of the servant's cabins scattered throughout the woods that enclosed the royal country estate outside Stockholm. Her father, Nels Peter Larson, was the King's chief gardener. As soon as Mabel, an only child, grew old enough, she joined her mother working at the palace. Her mother worked as a cook in the kitchen, and Mabel became a cleaning maid. Years later, their lives changed when Nels Larson accepted an offer to design the park system for the new, rapidly developing city of Chicago. When he sailed for America, the two women stayed in Sweden until he could send money for their ship's passage to join him in Illinois.

Mabel was perhaps eighteen when she and her mother boarded the steamer for New York City. A photo taken at the ship shows her looking up at the tall smokestacks and the fluttering flags. What was she thinking? Her light blonde-brown hair ruffled in the breeze, her soft youthful face smiled with an apprehensive excitement. She never had attended school and probably spoke no English. This might have been the first time she had been off the palace grounds. She was on her way to new opportunities. Her blue eyes must have sparkled in the misty spray as she stood on the deck searching the horizon for her first view of the Statue of Liberty and Ellis Island.

Nels Larson had secured employment for his wife and daughter in a boarding house for men who worked at a new greenhouse complex outside of Chicago. The owner of the greenhouse complex, Rudolph Scheffler, a young immigrant from Germany, was building his business by providing jobs and housing for inmates released from the state penal system. Along with room and board, Scheffler paid them a small wage in exchange for their labor. It proved to be a mutually beneficial arrangement. They were grateful for the job and worked hard, and in turn he treated them well. Scheffler also hired immigrant women to cook and clean at the boarding house.

There is much to admire about my grandfather, Rudy Scheffler. He left Germany as a young man, alone and with no money, and through hard work and determination, he built a small empire in the floral business in the Chicago area. But at least with his first wife and child, he did not behave admirably.

When the hot-blooded Rudy Scheffler met the pretty, shy Mabel, he stated his terms. Instead of just being the cook, her mother could be in charge of the boarding house with a good salary and living accommodations for both her and her husband Nels, on condition that Mabel become his wife. Otherwise, they could all leave. Mabel's parents convinced her of the advantages for this match, even the necessity. Rudy and Mabel were soon married.

In every aspect of his life, Rudy seized what he wanted. Mabel spoke bitterly of the brutality of their wedding night. She was a complete innocent, probably resistant and unresponsive to his overtures, and after that night she both feared and hated her husband. Nine months later when she gave birth to a girl instead of Rudy's desired son and continued to resist him in every way, he fired Mabel's mother, and filed for divorce from Mabel. Mother told me this first, but on another day, she shared with me her earliest memory, of being on the train with her parents. Were her parents still together, or just together on business that day, even though separated? Mother, just a young girl, wore a new fur-trimmed coat and hat, with a matching muff that she adored. When the train approached the station, her parents hurriedly gathered her up, not noticing her muff left behind on the seat. Not verbal yet, Mother remembers pointing and making noises trying to tell them, but they paid no attention to her. "The story of my life," she said ruefully.

It remains unknown to me how Mabel managed with her infant (my mother). Mother said that, after Mabel and Rudy divorced, Rudy gave Mabel no financial aid, and Mabel's parents refused to help her with housing or any other support. In their opinion, Mabel had failed everyone.

Mother wasn't clear on the following details, and I think what follows is accurate, but I'm uncertain of the sequence. Apparently, Rudy married the next boarding house cook, also an immigrant, who gave him Rudy Jr., his desired son. Rudy was heartbroken when his wife took their young three-year-old son to Germany to meet her parents, and the boy was trampled by run-away horses pulling a beer wagon.

Rudy divorced her immediately upon her return, and married another immigrant woman, whom he divorced after she produced only girls. Then he married Rose, one more immigrant woman. Rose, a devout Roman Catholic, gave him another daughter. Rudy appealed to the Bishop for an annulment, who refused, in spite of Rudy's promise of a large contribution to the church. A ruddy-cheeked, large-boned Irish Catholic, robust both physically and spiritually, Rose didn't take guff from anyone. Rudy had met his match. Soon she produced three sons. Always congenial and well liked, quick to laugh, Rose was also tough and expertly took over management of the business side while Rudy managed the greenhouses. She made it clear to him that, if he divorced her, she would take half of everything, as well as the children. Then she moved into her own bedroom. Rudy accepted his situation, developed his own personal life, and he and Rose lived together harmoniously.

The Scheffler floral complex provided handsomely for everyone, and Rudy and Rose trained their sons in the business. Through the years, the family maintained a respected and generous reputation in their community, and the children became popular and successful. Meanwhile, Rose also became a beloved pillar in her church. Rudy, who never stopped working, died of a heart attack at age ninety-three while driving a load of flowers into Chicago. His mistress, warmly befriended from the beginning by Rose, sat with the family at his funeral.

Their greenhouse complex was the sole—and very large—wholesale supplier for the burgeoning Chicago floral market, their substantial wealth multiplying during those pre-income-tax years. Rudy was very proud of his extensive spread of greenhouses. Though his former wives and their new husbands benefited by working in the expanding business, Mabel kept her distance. She nurtured her bitterness toward Rudy, and allowed it to spread to all men. She never remarried. She was a young woman, perhaps twenty, who was uneducated and barely spoke the language and, because of him, she was alone in a strange country, with a newborn she had never wanted.

Mother's work-roughened hands developed years before she and Daddy bought and restored the greenhouse in Marion. When she was ten, Mabel didn't have enough money to buy shoes or books for her daughter to attend 5th grade that autumn. Mabel contacted Rudy and gave Mother to him on his promise he would send her to school—a promise he had no intention of keeping. He turned his young child over to the boarding house cook.

When Rudy took Mother to meet this woman, Mother stood before the cook clutching her only possession, a beloved stuffed rabbit. The cook scoffed and snatched the old, worn rabbit from Mother's arms. "The first thing we'll do is get rid of this filthy thing," and threw it into the kitchen stove. When Mother cried out, the cook slapped her. "One thing I can't stand is a kid carrying on about nothing." She turned to Rudy. "What am I supposed to do with this God-dammed no-good filthy bitch?"

"Put her to work," Rudy replied, and walked away.

For the next four years, seven days a week, Mother scrubbed the floors of the large boarding house on her hands and knees. She never did them well enough to please the cook. "Bitch!" Cook would bellow through the house. "This floor is as filthy as you are—do it again." Mother repeated her scrubbing over and over, never understanding what she was doing wrong, but getting yelled at and slapped, nonetheless. "She never showed me how I was supposed to do it," Mother said.

"During those years, I don't remember anyone saying my name even once. I began to wonder if that was my real name: 'God-dammed no-good filthy bitch.'"

She ate with the hired men and slept alone in one of the upstairs bedrooms where the men's bedrooms were. She remained safe. No one would jeopardize his job by touching the boss's daughter. But I imagine they also felt sympathy for her. On her fourteenth birthday, Rudy reassigned her from working at the boarding house to working in the greenhouses with these men. They welcomed her protectively. These men knew her by her name, Gertrude, but they affectionately called her "Gert." She had lived all those years in the men's boarding house and had never been exposed to feminine or social graces, so she felt at home with their earthy ways. As she grew older she enjoyed joking and sharing a beer with them. She became "one of the guys."

Rudy's business was expanding rapidly. Mother, the only female and barely into her teens, worked alongside the men constructing additional greenhouses filled with the long, raised, shallow-box-like benches that would hold the growing plants. This required hauling first wheelbarrows of cement, bricks, and lumber for the structures, then wheelbarrows of soil and compost to fill the benches before they planted the seeds. Mother bragged she was able to keep up with the toughest. "I could out-work every one of them, and when I was old enough to drive, during bad weather I was the only one who could drive the delivery van the two-mile muddy road into town without getting stuck, not even once."

As I listened to Mother, I reached for her hand, looked into her face and said what a hard and sad life she had had, yet she had told me all this without a bit of anger or bitterness.

"Well, we're all just human, and do the best we can," she replied. We sat quietly.

"You're the most forgiving person I have ever known," I told her. She squeezed my hand, her eyes soft.

"And you're the most understanding.

This was Mother's life until she left to marry Henry. She didn't tell me how old she was then, but I think 19.

༄ ༄ ༄

The final months of Mother's journey were painful ones. Her osteoporosis continued relentlessly, compressing her spine in several places and causing her throat muscles also to collapse. It became harder for her to talk, and increasingly difficult for her to swallow food.

Could I find out before it was too late? The answer to the question that had haunted me since early childhood? One afternoon I asked her to please tell me why my birth had been such a disappointment. She turned her face to the wall and remained quiet for a long while. I feared she wouldn't tell, that I would never learn the truth. But then she turned back, looked at me, and began.

"Dad's hired men were good to me when I was a kid. Still, I was just one of the gang—never special to any one person. When I was twelve, I met a boy who became my best friend. With him, for the first time I learned what it felt like to have someone really care about me. He was always there when I needed him; he never let me down. For four years, we did everything together. His name was Robert, but he liked me to call him Robbie. I never had a friend like him again."

I first heard the name Robbie during college, the summer I worked as a camp counsellor, when my group of teenage girls gave me that nickname. It felt like a comfortable fit, so I kept it at the end of the summer. Mother's eyes widened when I told her my new name. From then on, she did call me Robbie, though her lips appeared awkward each time they shaped the word.

"Robbie was killed in a car accident the day before his fourteenth birthday, when I was sixteen." Mother continued. "Standing beside his casket, I swore to him that one day I would have a son. His name would be Robert, but I would call him Robbie."

When Mother told me this I stiffened, struggling to comprehend what she had said. Had this boy been the reason she rejected me from birth, accused me of being her greatest disappointment and never forgave me? The vein on the side of my forehead began to throb.

Her anguish as she shared this story, however, showed me the depth of her love for him. It might be difficult for me to understand the meaning of this friendship to her, an innocent, platonic adolescent passion. Yet her loving friendship with Robbie had given her something she had never experienced before—a relationship that lifted her from the neglect, abuse and loneliness, and gave her a loving experience that impacted her life so strongly that even after his death he continued to mean more to her than either of her husbands or any of her children ever would. She had completely loved Robbie, perhaps her one and only real love.

Seeing her with Henry, sitting in the car that night, showed me Mother was capable of passion. With my father, she had agreed to a marriage completely devoid of passion, and it was all wrong. When she became pregnant with me, did she develop the fantasy that if only she had a son and, in this way get her Robbie back, he would give her that bond of love again that would have allowed her to survive this disastrous marriage? When I was born a girl, her "most bitter disappointment ever," she lost all hope, plus she had broken her promise to Robbie. Resigned, she gave me his name. But her bitterness poisoned our relationship.

~ ~ ~

Because of her body's deterioration, eventually Mother couldn't lift her arms or move her body in any way, and it was hard for her to whisper a single word. Soon she became mute, completely helpless and bedfast. I sat with her every day, making sure she received timely pain medications to keep her as comfortable as possible. I had hung a bird feeder outside her window, and every morning we watched the birds fluttering in to eat. The amaryllis bulbs I planted along her window sill slowly unfolded into their full colors of red and purple. She liked me to brush her thin, wispy hair, which I did every day with a baby hair brush, cradling her head gently, then held a mirror so she could see how lovely she was. She had always longed for thick, beautiful hair. Now she seemed pleased with her own. James Herriot's stories became her favorite pastime, and I read them to her over and over to fill her hours

~ ~ ~

When Mother neared the end of her life, I urged Ellin to come, this time for herself. "You'll have regrets if you end it like this." She arrived the next day on the Greyhound Bus from Denver.

During Ellin's two-day visit, while Mother napped, she and I went to a nearby coffee shop. We sat together awkwardly, not having talked for so long. I broke our silence first, bringing up that day years ago that still pained me, when she and I had played in

Cobb's barn. "What a terrible ending to such a beautiful day," I murmured. "We were having so much fun, remember? Cobb must have phoned the folks and said he didn't want us playing in his barn, but why didn't Daddy simply tell us? We would have stopped. I can't understand why he got so mad." I paused, my words caught in my throat. "But he got mad only at you. We were both equally involved, more me than you even, for it was my idea in the beginning. Yet he beat you, then took Mother and me to the movies."

Ellin stared blankly. "Did that happen?" she asked. "I don't remember any of it. I do remember him beating me that time when I took the dime from their cash box. That's when he broke my tooth with a 2x4." She lifted her upper lip to reveal the still-present missing chunk. "But you know," she said brightly, "I'm fortunate that he cared that much about me, and he wasn't even my real father! I'm so grateful he did beat me, otherwise I probably would have grown up to become a thief."

This silenced me, though Ellin didn't seem to notice. Eyes downcast, she fidgeted with her cup. She said she had wanted to tell me some things for years. "You were so little when everything began. I'm sure you never knew what was going on." She stared at her cup, shuddered, took a deep breath and began the following story, not looking at me.

During the June when Marilyn turned twelve and she was nine, Henry, their real father, drove from Chicago to visit them. He had not seen them for year—even before Mother remarried. He said he wanted to get re-acquainted with his daughters, and Mother let him take Marilyn and her for a special outing. After all, she explained to them, he was their father and he had driven so far. He promised to buy them ice cream and pretty new dresses, things Mother and Daddy couldn't afford.

At first it was exciting. He did buy them dresses with twirly skirts, red with white ruffles for Marilyn, blue for Ellin to match her eyes. At the restaurant, he ordered delicacies they had dreamed of eating: double cheeseburgers with grilled onions and lots of dill pickles, and chocolate malts with real ice cream, so thick they had to eat them with spoons. "Would you like to see where I'm staying?" he asked.

They had never been to a hotel before. They tiptoed along the quiet hallways, fascinated when he had to open the door with a key, ignoring how he locked it behind them. It was like entering a secret playhouse. They touched the shiny-waxed chest of drawers, peeked into the bathroom with gleaming white fixtures. Henry let them bounce on the large, soft bed that had giant pillows with brown-patterned cases matching the bedspread. "Why don't you take off your pretty new dresses, so they won't get all wrinkled?"

Henry explained they were going to play a game that would help them understand how in a few years the three of them could make a lot of money together. He would teach them how to please a man, beginning with Marilyn, because he would save Ellin for big money one day. He instructed Ellin to kneel beside the bed to watch and learn, and to clutch her hands around his penis as he thrust in and out of Marilyn.

As the sun lowered in the western sky, they drove home, Marilyn huddled in the backseat, while Henry made Ellin lie across the front seat and hold his penis in her mouth. When Henry pulled into the driveway, Daddy strode out to the car. She and Marilyn ran to the house, so she didn't hear what the two men said, but she saw Daddy's anger. Did he suspect what Henry had done? She thought not, that he would have reacted differently. She thought he was telling Henry that he didn't want him there and not to come back.

Henry drove away and never returned to Marion again. Neither Daddy nor Mother asked them about their special day.

Nothing was ever said. Afterwards, however, everything changed. Marilyn and Ellin became withdrawn, sullen and fearful. They resisted Daddy whenever he offered to push them in their swing or even came near them. Frustrated, his neck muscles bulged, his face reddened. He began erupting into rages and vicious beatings. Mother, stricken, turned away, her body wilting with defeat. The few fun times they had shared together stopped. A quiet tension gripped the family. One day, when Ellin walked into our parent's bedroom to ask Mother a question, she saw a revolver in an open drawer. "Why do you have a gun?" she whispered.

"It's to keep skunks away," Mother answered through tightened lips. "Two-legged skunks."

Ellin now sat quietly weeping; I remained speechless, not wanting to believe what she was saying. Yet it shed light on so much of the tension that had hung on our family like a shroud, and how the beatings had begun. Our waitress approached and asked if we needed anything? Ellin ducked her head to hide the tears slipping down her cheeks. I assured the girl we were fine, but she refilled our cups. When she left, I handed my napkin to Ellin to replace her shredded one. She stared at the table, trembling. "I can hardly stand to remember this."

"Oh, Ellin—I'm so sorry." My words sounded inane and without comfort. She shrugged. "Thank you for telling me," I said. I reached for her hand, limp and unresponsive. She looked exhausted, dark lines beneath her eyes, shoulders sagging. I searched for something more to say but sat wooden, unable to find words. Over the years, at rare times, she had turned to me as her wise sister, in awe that I had a college degree. College couldn't prepare me for this. But she didn't seem to expect words; she only needed me to listen. I flooded with sorrow for what she and Marilyn had experienced, when they were so innocent and vulnerable, but also anger that neither Mother nor Daddy had protected or helped them. Our drinks had grown cold. "I think we've had enough of this for today," I said. "What would you like to do now? Mother should be awake, but we don't have to go back. I can just slip in quickly to tell her goodnight."

Ellin twisted her cup roughly round and round, droplets sloshing over the brim. She straightened. "No. She's expecting us. I'm okay. Let's go. We'll come back here tomorrow, and I'll finish. There's more. I want you to understand why it has been hard for me to see Mother." Pulling herself up, she crumpled the soggy napkin, dropping it into her full cup, and gathered her jacket along with her bulging, oversized purse. I hesitated. It wasn't a good moment, but Ellin and I had so few, we might not have any more, and I had wondered about this for so many years. Now, in light of what she had shared with me, I had to know.

"Before we go, could I ask you something?" Ellin said sure, and we sat back down. "Remember the time I was scalded in that pail of water when I was three? I have asked myself the question over and over whether I was pushed, or whether I fell? The few times I shared that incident with anyone they told me not to be naive, that of course Marilyn pushed me. Perhaps I am being naive, but I think that when Mother and Daddy heard my screams and came running, they must have seen Marilyn trying to pull me out of the bucket and concluded she was pushing me in."

Ellin nodded, confirming this, but quickly added that she hadn't been in the room the moment it happened. "That's what Daddy thought though, and he really beat Marilyn up."

Later I tried to put it all together, in the context of what Ellin had shared with me. It was the summer before my scalding the following March that she and Marilyn had had that terrible day with their father. On the day I was burned, I had presumed that Marilyn, only twelve years old, had thoughtlessly left the pail where she did to cool, probably thinking more about doing her hair than of the water. But now I could understand if she had seized that moment to avenge the horrors she was enduring—the recent rape by her father, and, then, when her behavior changed, her stepfather beating her while Mother turned away. During all that suffering there had been no one there for her. Yet, all these years, not knowing the whole story, my heart had told me that I fell all by myself, and I still believed it. Marilyn was the one trying to save me. For this once again she was misunderstood and beaten.

ᳫ ᳫ ᳫ

Mother opened her eyes when we walked through her door. The afternoon sun shone through the west-facing windows, onto her white sheets and into her face. Ellin lingered near the doorway, her determination to return fading. I touched her arm. "It's okay."

I asked Mother if the sun bothered her, would she like me to lower the shades? Her eyes told me no. She had grown so thin and always felt cold. I filled her water glass and spooned some into her mouth. "Did you have a nice nap?" I felt Ellin's presence behind me. I wanted to be by her side but continued making small talk to Mother, filling the silence. Ellin wandered over to sit on the windowsill in the sun. She crossed one leg over her other, folded white anklets drooping beneath her cuffed blue jeans. She smiled a lopsided grin at me, but quickly rested her elbow on her knee so she could cup her hand over her mouth, probably remembering her crooked and broken teeth.

We prepared to leave when the aide brought Mother's supper tray. Ellin approached her bed and spoke for the first time, with a forced cheerfulness: "You be a good girl now! I'll be back tomorrow."

Soon after, we found ourselves sitting in the parking lot. "I wish I knew what to say to you," I said.

"It's okay—there's nothing to say."

"So what would you like for dinner? Your choice, except I'm not eating a Big Mac. My heart suffered enough trauma today." We hooted, the tension dissipating. When she could afford it, Ellin's big treat was a Big Mac, while I refused to eat one—our ongoing playful argument.

"Okay, no Big Mac." She grinned at me. "But I want a good hamburger."

"I know just the place."

∽ ∽ ∽

The next day during Mother's afternoon nap Ellin and I returned to the coffee shop. After the waitress brought our steaming cups, Ellin took a sip of her coffee, and took a deep breath. "I need to finish this story before I leave. You probably never knew why Marilyn and I suddenly left home, and thought it was because Daddy and Marilyn were having so much trouble, but that had nothing to do with it." She lifted her cup but set it down without drinking, the cup shaking.

"When you visited me that time in Wichita for my birthday, I wanted to tell you, but while you were out of the room Mother warned me not to say one word to you." That autumn, when Ellin was fourteen and Marilyn sixteen, Henry wrote Mother and enclosed money for train tickets so the girls could visit him in Chicago. When Mother told them, they were stunned. She brushed aside their timid protests. "He hasn't seen you for years, and he is your father. It's nice that he wants to be with you again."

"She instructed us not to tell anyone," Ellin said. "I wanted to tell you before you left for school that day, but I was afraid to."

She took a deep breath and continued. Mother bought them new shoes, then packed peanut butter and grape jelly sandwiches into one of the shoeboxes, tying it with string. The three of them drove in silence to the station thirty miles away. "I can still feel those bristly train seats on my bare legs. We watched Mother wave good -bye as the train jerked into motion, and then looked at each other terrified. What was waiting for us?"

Henry met their train in Chicago the next day. He embraced them with big hugs, ignoring their resistance. At a restaurant, he encouraged them to order anything they wanted. "This is a celebration," he said. They picked at their food. "I have a big surprise. We're going to start making all that money I told you about years ago." He winked at Marilyn and bragged he had lined up some nice men for her the next day.

His smile widened when he turned to Ellin. "And you—you're going to win the big prize. You're going with a man who's paying me a lot of money. This is what I saved you for." He leaned toward them, grinning. "You're lucky to have a father who can arrange this for you. Your lives are going to change, you'll see. You're going to stay with me now and I'm going to buy you all kinds of pretty things." He drove to a seedy hotel and checked them into a room on the second floor, down the hall from his own. He instructed them to take baths and be beautiful for him in the morning.

"After he left, we huddled together on our bed whispering, afraid to even breathe," Ellin said. "We didn't know what we could do. He locked our door with a key from the outside, but even if we could get out, we had heard the hall boards creak. To reach the stairs, we would have had to pass his door and he might have heard us. Then we got an idea. We stripped our sheets, tied them together and knotted them to the bedpost, just like in stories. We opened our window, trying not to make a sound, and slid down, dropping to the sidewalk. Then did we run! We found a drugstore still open and rushed through the door sobbing and begging for help."

The clerk hurried them into a back room and called the police. The officers took them to Juvenile Hall where they told their story to a caseworker. She phoned our parents in the middle of the night. They decided they couldn't risk letting anyone know about this. Once they had purchased something from a competitor to their neighbor's business, and for several months these neighbors plus their friends boycotted the floral shop and the business floundered. That was minor compared to this. In our conservative small town, they feared this scandal could put them out of business.

༒ ༒ ༒

I understood too well about reputation in a small town. When I was a freshman in high school, the morning of our first dance, my date, one of the hill boys, met me at my locker. He shifted his eyes from the floor to the wall behind me, then to the ceiling as he apologized. "I'm really sorry," he said, "but I can't go with you tonight." I stammered and asked why? "When my parents found out I was taking you, they said no. They don't know you," he added quickly. "I know you're really nice and everything. It's because of your sisters. I'm really sorry."

I knew that when my sisters disappeared, they left behind what I only vaguely understood as "a bad reputation," although I had no idea what that meant. I was young, naive and innocent, and had known only that they had had few friends. I don't remember them ever going on a date. I knew they had not been popular but believed it had been because we lived in a shabby house in the wrong part of town, apart from the popular hill crowd. But I was painfully aware that our entire family lacked something. None of us fit in. We were socially isolated, lacked self-confidence and social skills, and had few friends.

I was the only one in our class who didn't attend the dance that night.

❧ ❧ ❧

When Daddy and Mother received that phone call from the Chicago police, Mother turned to Rose, her dad's wife. They lived in a suburb close to Chicago, and now Rose, always competent and with means, took over. She arranged for Marilyn, who was of legal age, to be put on a train to Idaho; she would live with her aunt there and finish high school. The police arrested Henry that night, and insisted that since she was underage, Ellin had to stay as their witness. They kept her in the Juvenile Detention Center for safekeeping until Henry's court hearing. After the trial, Rose, a devout Roman Catholic, paid for her to attend the Mt. Carmel Catholic Boarding School for Girls in Wichita to finish high school. Neither girl returned home.

"The folks were afraid we'd slip and say something that would ruin their business," Ellin said. "I'm sure they thought you'd make a mistake and say something too, that's why Mother insisted I not say anything to you." Her voice lowered, filled with sadness. "The day of the trial I had to testify against my father in court. Henry was sitting in the front row. I sat on a wooden chair beside the judge and tried not to look at him, but I felt his presence. Once when I glanced at him, he was staring at me with an expression of pure hatred."

During the preparation for the trial, additional information came out that helped the police link Henry to several unsolved cases of seductions and sexual assaults against underage girls. "But it was my testimony that sent him to prison." Her eyes filled with tears. "He was committed to the Illinois Prison for the Criminally Insane."

Meanwhile, Marilyn was in Idaho with her aunt, where she finished high school, then secured a job with a publishing house in Chicago. Bright and creative, she loved her job and advanced quickly. But when she was nineteen, she became pregnant with her eighteen-year-old boyfriend, George. In spite of his mother' outrage and attempts to block it, they married. They believed they were in love. Marilyn quit her job and they left Chicago and George's mother and moved to Denver, where George found menial work. They scrimped along, but when a daughter followed the birth of their son within a year, George returned to his mother.

Nursing my cup of tea, I listened to all of this with an increasingly sick feeling. At last I was beginning to understand those silences while I was growing up. All that time, until Mother took me with her to visit first Ellin and then Marilyn, I feared they were dead. After George abandoned Marilyn, she must have phoned Mother in desperation, which prompted our drive to Denver. But after our return home, again I fell into the silence and unknowing.

Ellin went through those long weeks in detention and the trial alone. The caseworker relayed Mother's message that even if she could scrape up the money to come, Daddy couldn't handle the business by himself during the busy autumn season. Mother never wrote to Ellin.

Ellin said Mother once told her that when Henry drove her home from the hospital after Ellin was born, he flew into a rage because Mother hadn't thanked him properly for taking care of Marilyn and the house while she was in the hospital. When she got out of the car to carry her baby into the house, Henry revved the car across the lawn, trying to run them both down. Somehow Mother escaped and got to her father.

From the beginning, Grampa had pegged Henry as a handsome but no-good con man, but Mother ignored his warnings;

she had fallen under Henry's spell. When she married him, her father banished them both. Nevertheless, after Mother, clutching her newborn, escaped Henry, her father relented, and both took her in and gave her the job in his business office.

To Mother's alarm, Henry kept Marilyn, who was eighteen months old, for more than a year. Mother believed he used her sexually. Whether or not that was true, I don't know. I imagine Rudy took Mother back on the condition that she divorce Henry, and Rudy probably paid for it. I wondered—if not for her father, would she have returned to Henry?

It was painful to hear that Mother never went to Chicago to be with Ellin nor gave her any kind of support. In the court room, she would have had to listen to her daughter tell what had happened to them, including that Mother had sent them alone by train to Henry. She would have seen Henry and heard him sentenced to prison. What agony of conflict she must have suffered. In spite of realizing he was a two-legged skunk who deserved to be shot, handsome, seductive, smooth-talking Henry still held Mother captive.

Ellin continued. "After all this time, I decided to attend my class reunion in Marion two years ago." Surprised to see her, one of her former classmates asked if she had kept her baby? "Everyone assumed I dropped out of school and disappeared because I was pregnant." Ellin laughed through tears, shaking her head in disbelief. "Me, pregnant? I was so shy and withdrawn, I never even touched a boy."

Marilyn and Ellin never saw their father again. After he was released from prison, he didn't contact them. Several years later, Mother received word: while on a train on his way to his sister in Idaho, Henry had died from a stroke. She telephoned the funeral details to the girls. Mother couldn't go, but she thought the girls should. She became upset when they refused, scolding them for not wanting to say goodbye to their own father. "I said goodbye to him long ago," Ellin told me bitterly.

~ ~ ~

I sat thinking about all that Ellin had told me during these two days, trying to digest it along with everything I had learned from Mother. All of it made my heart ache; I felt deep compassion for all three of them. It wasn't a matter of who was responsible, who to blame. Each of them had her own story; each of them had suffered terribly their entire lives.

Perhaps as their mother one would hold her more responsible. She was the adult. They were her innocent and vulnerable children. I wish she had had a different childhood herself so she could have been a different Mother to all of us. Now I better understood Mother's behavior as a Mother, so many times unbelievably cruel and emotionally disconnected. She didn't know anything else. She treated her children as she had been treated as a child. As an adult, she was still a wounded child herself, unable to be more. She had never once experienced the loving touch of a mother nor any relationship with women, or men, that would have helped her develop an ability to express affection or feminine softness, even the most meagre of mothering skills. No one had been there to help her, to heal her suffering as a child. Only with the seductive, con-man Henry did she feel lust and being wanted, but this only led to more suffering for her.

Her response that day to Marilyn, sobbing in despair with two babies in that Denver attic, reflected Mother's overwhelming sense of helplessness and failure, which she seldom showed but with which she suffered deeply. After we returned home, I would see her sitting alone, deep in thought, her face tortured and sorrowful. She didn't have money to bale Marilyn out. She couldn't bundle them up and take the three of them home, couldn't hope for any support from Daddy or our conservative small town, and she had no friends or family she could turn to. She wouldn't have had any idea about possible resources in Denver. And tragically, it would never even have occurred to Mother to simply hold her daughter and weep together. No one had ever touched her lovingly or let her cry in their arms. When she drove away I'm certain her heart was breaking, but the only way she knew to handle heartbreak was how she had been forced to handle it herself growing up: suck it up, snap on your stoicism and cold armor that blocks the pain, and get to work.

All of this, however, didn't lessen my sorrow for my sisters. Neither of them, so innocent and vulnerable, had a chance from birth onward. They had never had anyone there for them either.

Theirs was a story of overwhelming suffering and sorrow. I could only hold all three of them in my heart. No judgments. Just an acceptance of what is, held with compassion.

❧ ❧ ❧

After we left the coffee shop, Ellin asked to see Mother alone this last time before she returned to Denver. Although I felt uneasy hearing the determined tone in her request, I dropped her off. Later she confessed that during her time with Mother, she described to her in detail what happened to them when Henry took them for the day, when they were just twelve and nine years old. "I thought she should know before she died what he did to us in that hotel room."

I filled with anger and regret. Why had I left her alone with Mother? Even though what happened to my sisters had been horrific, with only days to live Mother lay bedfast unable to move or speak even a word. To confront her now seemed cruel, like kicking a dying, defenseless animal. Mother's and my relationship had changed. I now felt strongly protective of her. Couldn't her final hours be peaceful? Had Ellin needed to wait until Mother became helpless and unable to answer back before confronting her with this? Did she really need this revenge?

Yet my anger melted as I looked into her face, and I knew that whatever her reasons, she had had the right to do this. That terrifying experience had damaged my sisters irreparably. Both she and Marilyn had suffered over and over from Mother's neglect. I hoped her saying this to Mother, and also to me, now gave Ellin a bit of closure. I imagined Mother had already known everything she told her anyway.

During the days following Ellin's departure, I continued to digest everything that both she and Mother had told me. It shed light on so much. At last those suffocating silences were explained, the carefully guarded mysteries revealed. As I began to put all the pieces together, I understood—at least in my mind—that none of the family's suffering had ever been my fault. All these years, even though Mother's accusations never made sense and left me confused, still, since childhood, I had carried this guilt, convinced I must be responsible in some way I just couldn't grasp. As a dependent and vulnerable child, you believe what you're told by your mother, especially something this critical. I had suffered with this my entire life. Now, sitting at Mother's bedside while she slept, I began to feel the heaviness fall away. I was never the one responsible. The beatings and sobs and broken lives, all of our family's pain, the shunning I endured in our community. None of it, none of it, was ever my fault. I found myself repeating this over and over to myself, becoming tearful as the magnitude began to sink in. Life-long thoughts and beliefs don't shift quickly, but slowly, over time, I came to peace in my heart as well as my mind with my truth.

⸿ ⸿ ⸿

As Mother's swallowing became difficult, I tipped pureed food down her throat, wiped the dribbles from her chin, and repeated this again and again. If she couldn't eat, the only alternative, other than natural death, was for the medical staff to insert a feeding tube into her stomach. By Kansas law, once inserted it could not be removed until her death, regardless of whether the patient lay comatose for years, regardless of any legal plea filed by the family. Before choosing Mother's nursing home, I made certain it was one where we could make this choice. Some homes, for religious convictions, or simply moral reasons, did not allow a choice, and routinely inserted the feeding tube when the person could no longer eat. They explained they could not allow anyone in their care to starve to death. I learned that without the tube, if the person was kept hydrated and peaceful, he or she died a pain-free and natural death. Mother's staff even offered to circle the dying person's bed with the family and sing or pray together.

When Mother first entered this wing of the nursing home, the director apologized for the temporary lack of a private room. Mother's roommate had lain in a coma for almost three years. When the moment of decision had had to be made about whether to insert a feeding tube or not, her daughter hysterically demanded it, unable to allow her mother to die. Her mother soon lapsed into the coma, and the daughter had not visited for more than two years. When the director explained this to both of us, Mother turned to me with pleading eyes. I squeezed her hand and promised.

During this long final year, our hours together had become gentle and tender to us both. Mother had become the dependent child; I had become her nurturing Mother. I'm certain my loving care was the first she had experienced in her life. Though this was a demanding role that left me exhausted every night, it allowed me to experience my mother in a new way. Our hearts had softened, without our even noticing. The moment came when I no longer saw even a shred of the Mother of my childhood lying in that bed before me, but a defeated, suffering and scared human being—and my heart broke completely open. Our last days together became precious.

One night when I said goodnight to Mother, I didn't know it would be our final time together. I leaned down to her in her wheelchair and kissed her cheek. "I love you, Mother. I'm so thankful you're my mother."

She tilted her face up to mine. I stared at her. Her face glowed, her eyes luminous with pure love. Not until later did I realize she was transitioning. Smiling, she effortlessly, tenderly, reached up her arm she had been unable to move and caressed my cheek. Clear words came from her throat that had been unable to utter even a whisper: "I was never mad at you."

During that night she died, a peaceful smile on her face. But before she departed, she had given me what I had yearned for all my life.

Although I have regrets giving up those seven years, especially my university program I so loved, I have never once had the slightest doubt that I made the right choice. I would have missed the experience that gave me my mother, and through her, my self.

Legacy

After growing up in this family, how did the future unfold for my sisters and me? In this chapter, I have gathered together a brief summary to share with you—our legacy.

Ellin and I lived thirty-five miles from each other for the last sixteen years and although I tried to get together several times, she preferred to remain reclusive. After she left home—years later when we were both adults and I found her again—our relationship had been like this. We connected for brief moments during life's critical incidents, then Ellin would withdraw into her private world. She married young and had three daughters before her divorce. She did her best to care for her children but overwhelmed with her own needs, she often was distant from them as well. Though she remained a social loner, she held a responsible job as an auditor for the State of Colorado, until she took early retirement at age 55. After her retirement, she devoted her time to writing—first religious music and then a translation of the Bible—having felt a calling to do both. Though she hoped to publish her efforts, she remained unsuccessful. I felt concerned about her through the years, but she gave me little choice but to honor her need to be alone.

After only rare and brief contacts between us since 1999 when she came to say goodbye to Mother in the nursing home, in July 2018, I received a phone call from her daughter, telling me that Ellin had been admitted to hospice care in Denver, and she had only a brief time to live. She had asked for me.

I sat beside Ellin in her hospice bed. Her daughter had warned me that Ellin slept most of the time and was unable to speak more than a word or two. After some time, I spoke her name softly several times. She opened her eyes, focused on me, and hoarsely said my name. We clasped hands, our eyes holding each other. As I looked at this shriveled and broken woman, my heart wrenched, feeling anguish for the difficult life she had endured. I suddenly became too overcome with emotion to say anything. There were so many things I wanted to tell her, but I was unable to speak. We sat silently, yet—during those moments together, until she fell back asleep—we felt each other's love. She died two days later.

Before I received the news of Ellin's death, I had planned to visit her again at the hospice and asked her daughter if there was anything I could take to her that she would enjoy? She told me Ellin's favorite flavor ice cream was vanilla-bean, and she would love that. When I learned she had died, I bought a vanilla-bean ice cream cone and sat under a tree in the park where she and I could enjoy it together. I told her, then, what I had wanted to say when I returned to visit her in the hospice: that she was never responsible for any of her suffering. None of it was her fault. She was a beautiful, innocent young girl who had deserved to be loved, cared for and protected. I also told her how glad I was that she was my sister and how much I loved her. I felt her presence sitting beside me, absorbing my words. It was a precious moment. I know at last she is at peace, embraced into the unconditional love she always deserved.

Marilyn died in March 2010, three months before her 85th birthday. (Ellin gave me this information a year and a half later). I know nothing about her cause of death and little about her life after we lost contact more than fifty years ago—only the following snippets and scraps of information Ellin shared with me in 1999, shortly before Mother's death. From these, I have filled in my own assumptions.

After George left Marilyn, in her early twenties with two small children, she remained in Denver and struggled with poverty and depression. George joined the army, however, so Marilyn received a meagre but lifesaving allotment from the government for his two children. To make ends meet, she let men move in with her both to share the finances and to provide companionship. First one man then a second lived with her for brief times, but both disappeared when both times she became pregnant. After the birth of these two men's sons, she turned away from men. She survived on welfare and tried to find work she could do from home, but her attempts to earn money failed.

She joined a nondenominational church that met in a neighborhood garage where members worked themselves into a religious frenzy, speaking odd sounding syllables they claimed was the biblical speaking in tongues. She left that group and became a "born again" member of a large and popular church where her religious zeal consumed her, but over time she drifted away into her own private misery. I imagine she concluded, like Mother before her, that even God had abandoned her.

Marilyn suffered from a clinical depression that grew through the years. Several visits to the army hospital clinic provided no relief. She had three boys and one girl. At an early age, her daughter chose to live in Germany with her father, who had remarried and was stationed there with the army. Although Ellin had no specific information, she thought the girl did all right. As Marilyn's sons eventually left, she lost everything and withdrew into an isolation dictated by poverty. Although I have no information about the childhoods of Marilyn's sons, with her own childhood experience of incest and violence, and realizing her lack of support and the pressures she was enduring as a single mother living in poverty, I can only imagine she parented in a similar way she had experienced, the only way she knew.

Marilyn's third child, a son, was her pride. He completed college and became a pilot for one of the major airlines. Her other children looked up to him as their hero. I imagine she viewed him and his accomplishments as reassurance that she had not failed at everything. She must have loved the fact that he had gone to college as she had wanted to, and that he had found a way to escape the world's hardships by soaring into the skies. Did she believe his success would be the inspiration and guide to his siblings to find their pathway to security and freedom?

His suicide devastated everyone and thrust Marilyn into a darkness from which she never emerged. I never met him, and will never know what broke inside him. Her youngest son, either before or after his brother's suicide, was sentenced to prison for murder. (I believe this to be accurate. I wrote to Ellin for confirmation but my letter was returned: "Attempted—Not known—Unable to Forward.")

Years later, Ellin's grandson committed suicide, a bright young man who had completed law school, plus a second graduate degree in business. Though he hid it well, he suffered from depression, and remained a social loner in spite of a comfortable social façade. He married and held a responsible job in the corporate business world. He did tell me that he had suffered sexual abuse and other forms of violence that began during his pre-school years. In spite of my urging, he refused to seek help and insisted he was fine reading his "self-help" books.

All of this painful family history makes it even harder for me to understand why Marilyn chose to live. Eventually, homeless and in dire poverty, she found shelter on the outskirts of Denver in an abandoned house trailer without utilities. I can't imagine how she survived day by day, including through our Colorado winters. She kept her son's ashes with her for years before arranging for his burial in a cemetery. Once a year, on the anniversary of his death, the cemetery officials observed a woman place a handful of wildflowers on his gravesite. For two years on that date, Ellin waited at the cemetery hoping to find Marilyn but never did. Then one day, when the bus she was riding stopped for a red light, Ellin saw her. Marilyn was scavenging through a trash barrel, her clothes in tatters, broken shoes tied onto her swollen feet with rope. Ellin never saw her again.

I reflect on these events, rippling down from generation to generation—women trapped in their naiveté and innocence, unknowingly establishing patterns etched deeply into the familial unconscious. Generations of women who did their best, but, caught in the vicissitudes of their lives, made poor choices, and experienced continuing betrayal, abandonment, and suffering.

Although my marriage didn't last forever, my former husband and I were married for almost forty years and stayed trusted friends. Neither of us remarried, and I remained at his side supporting him so often that many people didn't realize we had separated. We had two children (a son and a daughter), and five grandchildren (two boys and three girls), all of whom have always been precious to both of us.

When Roy's health began to fail, our daughter and I managed his care. As his health declined, he transferred full ownership and responsibility for his company to her. She now leads it forward into the next phase, committed to, and holding sacred, his founding principles. Our son chose to follow his own interests and continues to do well.

I'm so glad Roy lived to see that his dream—not only was fulfilled—but lives on. Most of our family were at his bedside when he peacefully died in 2013, pain free and conscious, unable to speak but able to hear our final words to him.

My son and his family continue to live in Kansas City. He has grown into a fine man who is a committed husband and a devoted father to his two successful and beautiful children.

When our daughter and her family moved to Colorado, I followed them, continuing my close relationship with her and my grandchildren. My daughter enjoys a loving relationship with her husband, and her three children reflect her positive mothering.

‿‿‿

A week after Mother's death, while I sat writing in my journal, she suddenly appeared. I felt her strong presence, and she told me—in clear words, though they weren't audible—that it has been important for me to learn I am not responsible for everyone's suffering in our family. The problems of my sisters had more to do with her, not me. For years, I have felt the support and guidance from a strong internal presence I call my Spirit Guide. I seldom speak of this with anyone, and never did with Mother. Now Mother told me she would always be with me, that I can turn to her for help, for she and what I call my Spirit Guide are the same—part of the universal feminine energy. I started to ask her a question about my sisters, but she faded away.

‿‿‿

Five years later, in February 2005, my beloved dog, Spencer, died. I had gotten him soon after Mother's death and he had been my closet companion through those painful years when I began to put my life together, following not only Mother's death but also my divorce. I had reluctantly agreed for my lawn man to spray small patches of weeds in my front yard, a toxic spray, and—although it was not near the backyard where Spencer romped—I believed it was responsible for his cancer. My grief was inconsolable, a grief that encompassed all my losses.

My therapist encouraged me to contact a medium he knew to be reputable, to clarify whether I was responsible for Spencer's death. I felt skeptical and viewed this as quackery, but I called for an appointment. I was put on the medium's five-month wait list. I received a call two days later that she had a cancellation. "You sounded in such distress, we're offering it to you," her manager said. The next day, on February 21st, we had our phone session.

"Oh my—lots of people are tumbling into line wanting to tell you things!" the medium laughed. "Your father is first. He said it's significant you're having this session today—it's his birthday." I had forgotten. "He wants you to know how much he regrets never telling you that he loved you; he realizes it would have helped. He also wants you to know there was something wrong with his head." I remained mute. Could I have asked what had been wrong? "Your mother is eager for you to know she made peace with her sister M." Mother had always been close to her half-sister Myrtle in Illinois. Did she mean her mother, Mabel? But no, it must be Marilyn.

"There's a darling little boy dashing around," the medium said, "who is about five or six years old, with black curly hair and mischievous eyes. He says he lived with you and always knew you loved him. He wants you to know how much it meant to him that you were with him when he died. He had something wrong with his heart and was in pain. As soon as he passed over, he saw lots of rainbows and didn't hurt anymore. He knows you miss him, and he's sending you a brother and sister. They will not arrive together. The sister will come later." She paused. "Do you care for foster children?"

I confessed that I had asked for this appointment because of the loss of my dog. I had been afraid, if I told her that, she'd not agree to work with me. He was a five-year-old black, curly-haired standard poodle and very energetic.

"Oh, now I understand! I have many people ask for a session after the loss of a special pet. He's rushing up, wanting you to know that the pesticide had nothing to do with his illness." I hadn't mentioned the pesticide. "He was an angel, who came to be with you during a particularly difficult time in your life. It was written in the book, (he's running to get it to show me), that the plan from the beginning was that he would leave you on February 13th." On February 13th, during our appointment, my veterinarian and I decided to put Spencer to sleep the next morning. I asked to have that last night with him but while still in her office, Spencer had a sudden spasm of pain, making me realize the extent of his suffering. I asked her to do it immediately, and I stayed with him during the process. "Even though you didn't feel ready for him to leave, one day you'll understand that the timing was right. He will continue to be with you even though he won't return again."

Two months after my session I acquired a black standard poodle puppy, that I named Nicolas. I inquired whether he had a sister. He had just one, and I contacted the breeder in Kansas City who had taken her. She told me she had placed the dog with a trainer in Texas to prepare her to become a show dog. She was gone. A year and a half later I received a call from this breeder, who told me a repairman had seen the numerous crates of dogs in her basement and reported her to authorities. They were coming the next day. She had to get rid of a lot of dogs quickly and did I want some?

Within the hour I got in my car and drove the 650 miles to her home in Kansas City. I brought back two dogs, and found a good home for one, but kept the one who was underweight, damaged and terrified. Sweet and timid by nature, despite harsh force by her trainer, she had failed to develop into a dog that would strut in a show ring. She had been returned to the breeder, and—for more than a year—had been abandoned to a crate in the basement, alongside the crates of the other failures. This dog was Nicolas's sister, and I named her Amy.

"But," continued the medium, "there is someone else here who wants to tell you something. His name is Robbie, too. He was killed in a car accident when he was thirteen. He knows his death made your life much harder, and he wants you to know that he has been looking out for you."

I sat very still. As long as I can remember, I have felt a strong, protective presence—very real, and separate from my Spirit Guide. For many years I was naive and unaware, putting myself in dangerous situations: as a child growing up, often wandering alone; as a college student, walking to a night job across an isolated and darkened campus, chased once by a man I outran; and, when I interned professionally as a social worker, going alone into dangerous and unsafe environments. Reflecting back, I'm astonished I was never harmed. Now, I overflowed with gratitude to this young boy, Robbie, Mother's best friend, who has been with me, looking out for me, all this time.

The medium drew our session to a close: "All of them want to encourage you to play your violin."

What? I had wanted to play violin for years as a young girl but there was no opportunity for violin lessons in my town. I had been assigned a clarinet by our band director, grew to love this instrument, and at age sixteen began lessons at a nearby college. That summer I also began lessons on the violin there. I had saved enough money to buy a used one. I wanted to play both instruments.

At the end of the summer, my violin teacher enthused that I had covered in three months what he would expect in a year. I shared this with our minister, expecting him to echo my excitement. He told me I was being foolish. It was too late to begin a new instrument, especially when I was doing so well on the clarinet. I trusted his judgment more than my heart, and quit playing the violin. How often I have regretted that decision. Too late at age sixteen?

"Now it's too late for me to pick up a violin," I told the medium, then added hesitantly: "What I have wanted to do is write, but I'm afraid it's too late for that as well. I missed my chance."

"No. No! That's it! That's the violin. And it's not too late. You have time yet. They hope you will do it."

After the close of our session, I tearfully reflected on all that I had learned. How thin the veil is between us and those who have passed over. They remain strong, unseen forces in our lives, even though we are often unaware of them. I remember another time, not so long ago, when such unseen forces became clear to me. I had returned to Marion to take care of some business and to tend my parents' graves. Before I left, I drove through our family's old neighborhood, noticing all the changes through the years.

Ellin and I never returned to Cobb's barn together. I got out of my car and walked across his deserted property. Overgrown with weeds, his house had been torn down, but the stone barn remained. Inside, I climbed the wobbling ladder and pushed open the trapdoor into the hayloft. Lying on the floor, fallen out of the cupola, was the board seat. Cobwebs dangled among layers of dirt, and a new generation of pigeons rustled their feathers warily on rafters thick with droppings. I stood in the moldy shadows, feeling the dampness of old stone, and listened for echoes of that June day so many years ago, a day that had begun so sweetly but ended so painfully wrong. Our rope, faded and frayed, hung from the rafter.

I drove down the gravel lane to the railroad tracks, and got out of my car to walk, gripped by the memory of that day when I was nine years old and had gone to find the woman and her baby in the boxcar. Shading my eyes against the glare of the sun, my nostrils prickled with the acrid odor of hot tar. Screams of locusts pierced through the stillness. I saw the rails, rusted now, lying among weeds, stretching to nowhere.

Through these years, I had believed I was driven to find that woman and baby out of my guilt for growing up the spared child, watching my father beat my step sisters. However, in those moments at our supper table, listening to him explain why the woman and baby had been banished to a gurney in the hallway behind the hospital's entrance door, I awakened to the prejudice and injustice not only within him and our family, but in our community. Now, as I stood gazing down those tracks, once again feeling the ache in my heart, I understood it had been something different. As a little girl, watching that mother cradle and protect her newborn, a baby born in the same room as I had been, my mother refusing to even touch me, I didn't see dark skin or their suffering, nor did I even think of my sisters. I envied that little girl.

Driving back to our street, before leaving town I paused in front of our former property. Everything in that entire section of our block had been torn down and replaced, except for Cobb's abandoned stone barn, at the back of the field adjoining our property. I looked across toward our island. The inner meadow there had become a working field, native grasses and wildflowers succumbing to the plow. The Conservation Corps of Engineers had dredged and re-channeled waters to prevent flooding. The creek would have been changed; trees would have been felled. Nothing would be the same—but I couldn't say for sure that my childhood experiences on that magical island were as I remember. How do we embellish memory when we grow up trying to escape our lives? I could face the dangling, frayed rope in Cobb's hayloft, the torn-down buildings, even the weed-infested, idle, railroad tracks. But I couldn't shatter my eight-year-old's fantasy of that magical kingdom, too precious within my memories. I couldn't return to Dogfish Island.

As I sat pondering our lives as a family, an astonishing thing happened: a black mist appeared, live glittering particles that shaped into an arc to hover above Cobb's barn and extend across five acres right over where our house once stood. It slowly darkened, like an ebony rainbow. I blinked, and turned my eyes away, but when I looked back, it was still there. I drove to the end of the street, turned off the car and sat frozen in wonder and disbelief. When I returned, the jet-black mist had disappeared, but then it came back, exactly as before, and remained in the air.

Staring at this shimmering black arc, I realized I was being given a gift— I was allowed to see the manifestation of that dark energy that held my family captive. My parents fought with this darkness, but in spite of all their good intentions, they became ensnared in its tenacious grip—good persons hungry for love, but defeated, unable to give or receive it.

I turned the key and drove away.

◌ ◌ ◌

And so, I pick up a pen instead of a bow. It's not the same, of course, but writing has some advantages over a violin. It's easier to slip a notebook into my purse, and at any hour, almost anywhere, I can open it and write. But I went a step further. After all these years, I applied to a low residency MFA program in creative writing and, while there, I began to write this memoir. Whether or not I could have progressed earlier in the fields of writing or academia, I'll never know. It's too late now for me to become accomplished in either one, but I accept my decisions. My life is filled with other rich gifts and picking up my pen just for my own pleasure is enough.

My intention with this memoir has been to tell the stories of the members of my family, most of whose voices were misunderstood and silenced. My pen was the only voice they had left. As I wrote, my prayer every day was that my pen would serve as a hollow quill through which their words could flow. Feeling their presence, during the entire process, I trust this has been so.

~ ~ ~

In 2012, our family gathered for a special event in a ballroom with a wall of windows that overlooks the Flat Irons Range of the Rocky Mountains. Our city of Boulder spreads along the plateau sheltered at its base. These mountains are a majestic range, undulating up from the prairie to form the lower foothills, so popular among hikers and campers, then gradually rise higher and higher, each tier more rugged with the boulders that give both the mountains and our city their name. This range of mountains dominates our lives and serves to remind me every day of that sheltering presence within me, indomitable and eternal, yet as close and gentle as my breath.

I see my daughter with her fifteen-year-old daughter, standing across from me in the ballroom, chattering and laughing, each exuding a presence so secure and beautiful. My heart filled with awe and gratitude. We are frail human beings living in a challenging world, and we'll experience our shares of heartaches, but that crushing cycle of violence and suffering that dominated my family for generations has been broken. All of my grandchildren feel secure and loved in their homes and will never need to flee to neighbors' houses or an isolated island to seek safety from physical abuse. As evidenced by my first night home from the hospital as an infant and the dream I had about that night years later, I came into this world with a spirit determined both to survive and to bring love to our family. From a very early age I reached out to find a more loving way to live than I was experiencing. Many generous hearted kind people responded, nurturing me as I grew. All of this prepared me to nurture my own children differently from the way my sisters and I were treated in our home.

Now I watch my daughter carrying this unconditional love forward even stronger, passing it on to her children, and through them, to our generations of the future.

The new story has begun

Acknowledgments

I have so many people to thank for supporting my quest to learn the craft of writing, and beyond, to learn how writers create works of art with their words.

It must begin with the University of Iowa's Summer Writing Festival, where I took my first seminar in 1994, taught by Mary Nilsen. For several summers, I returned to study with Mary, during which our friendship developed and deepened. After all these years, Mary, who founded and owns Zion Publishing, is publishing my memoir, the sweetest possible culmination of our relationship. Working with Mary as my midwife, helping me birth my manuscript into an actual, beautiful book, has been one of the joys of my life.

I took every seminar that I could, also, with Marilyn Abildskov, another excellent teacher who became my friend, who encouraged me to go for my MFA in writing, and wrote a letter supporting my application. This memoir began because of you.

Other outstanding teachers with that program taught me through the years, especially Nancy Barry, Sands Hall, and Christine Hemp. I owe each one of you so much.

Being accepted by the Vermont College of Fine Arts for my MFA in writing, under the leadership of Louise Crawley, became the realization of my long-deferred dream. There I had the good fortune to work with several outstanding teachers, published writers themselves, who also have a gift for teaching the craft:

Sue William Silverman, who first welcomed me to the program, then patiently, richly, began introducing me to what creative nonfiction is all about. Your excellent teaching inspires me still.

Sascha Feinstein, whose joyful spirit and unwavering belief in me gave me the courage to begin this memoir after insisting I write it, and has whole-heartedly supported my progress from the beginning to the end.

Laurie Alberts, whose expertise inspired, guided and supported me as a teacher while in the program, then later generously helped me to the finished product. How grateful I am for your friendship, your keen insight, warmth, and caring touch.

Christina Baldwin, who early on gave me warm support in her writing seminar on Whidbey Island, when I didn't think I could find the courage to move from secret keeper to secret revealer. For the first time, with you, I shared the bones of my story aloud and knew I could then write it.

Ruth Ozeki and Linda Solomon, leaders of our summer Hollyhock writing seminar, who warmly encouraged me, and supported my desire to go beyond just telling my own story. "Yes, tell everyone's story, let us weep for everyone." And I did. Ruth later graciously read my manuscript and offered helpful suggestions.

Errol Schubot, PhD, dear friend and therapist, who guided me along the challenging path of healing from this childhood. Without our work together, I would never have been able to write this story.

Kaelin Kelly, certified Energy Practitioner, EEM-CLP, who worked with me for three years balancing my energy, which had been scrambled during my childhood, creating the clarity of thought that helped me organize, write, and complete this memoir. How much I owe you.

Jim Yensan, good friend, meditation teacher, and Apple expert. You straightened out my computer frustrations over and over with the patience and good humor of a Buddha.

And lastly my family, who supported my every dream:

Roy, my husband and friend. From the beginning, you supported my wish to write, when I didn't even know how to begin. Even though now deceased, I know you would be glad to know that my dream also came true.

My son David and his children, Ariana and Remington. I love you and carry each of you forever in my heart.

Ashley, Gareth, and Kiana Grace. During my graduation ceremony, when I received my MFA in writing at age 76, you sat on the front row holding posters: "Our GHG rocks!" Your "Gray-haired Granny" hopes you always remember that it's never too late to go for your dream. I love you completely, forever and ever.

And first and finally, my beloved daughter, Linda, without whom my healing journey never would have begun, and without which I couldn't have written this story. Know always how thankful and blessed I am for the gift of sharing this life's journey together with you. I could only dedicate my book to you.

ROBBIE DUNLAP retired to an old farm house she remodeled in rural Colorado, where she lives with her standard poodle, surrounded by her gardens and bird sanctuary. She fills her days writing, reading, and gardening, secure in the knowledge that her nearby daughter and grand -children are reaping the rewards of unconditional love.

www.ingramcontent.com/pod-product-compliance
Lightning Source LLC
Chambersburg PA
CBHW072341090426
42741CB00012B/2869